COACHING YOUTH GYMNASTICS

An Essential Guide for Coaches, Parents and Teachers

Lloyd Readhead

D0731656

THE CROWOOD PRESS

First published in 2016 by
The Crowood Press Ltd
Ramsbury, Marlborough
Wiltshire SN8 2HR

www.crowood.com

© Lloyd Readhead 2016

British Library Cataloguing-in-Publication Data
A catalogue record for this book is available from the British Library.

ISBN 978 1 78500 220 5

Illustrations by Lloyd Readhead

Photographs by Alan Edwards

Typeset by Jean Cussons Typesetting, Diss, Norfolk

Printed and bound in India by Replika Press Pvt Ltd

CONTENTS

Preface   4

1   An Introduction to Gymnastics   6
2   The Benefits of Participating in Sport   13
3   The Role of the Coach   17
4   The Principles of Learning   24
5   How to Coach   29
6   Sports Psychology   43
7   Planning the Training   48
8   Developing Range of Movement   54
9   Developing Strength and Endurance   62
10 Guidelines for Good Coaching Practice   72
11 Understanding Biomechanical Principles   77
12 Coaching the Generic Foundation Skills   88
13 Coaching Floor Exercise Skills   98
14 Coaching Vault   123
15 Coaching Asymmetric Bars/Uneven Bars   138
16 Coaching Balance Beam   150
17 Coaching Men's Artistic Gymnastic Skills   153
18 Coaching Rings   160
19 Coaching the Parallel Bars   167
20 Coaching the Horizontal Bar   175
21 Preparing for Competitions   183

    Useful Information   189
    Glossary of Terms   190
    Index   192

PREFACE

The sport of gymnastics is growing in popularity and has achieved great success in recent years. There are a number of factors that have contributed to this success. These include an excellent talent identification and talent development system; a first-rate coach education and coach development programme; a rise in the number of full-time dedicated gymnastic centres; an increase in the number of paid professional coaches; and training grants for gymnasts. These are supported by an excellent team of back-up staff and, of course, by considerable investment from lottery funding.

Gymnastics has recently gained a great deal of positive media coverage on television

Beth Tweddle: Multi gold medal winner at World and European Championships and winner of Dancing On Ice.

and through the newspapers. This increase in coverage is a direct result of British gymnasts winning medals at the Commonwealth Games and at the European, World, and Olympic Championships.

Another popular source of media coverage is the light entertainment television industry. Popular shows such as *Strictly Come Dancing*, *Dancing On Ice*, *Tumble* and *Britain's Got Talent* have been watched by millions of viewers. The winners of these programmes have all included a number of gymnasts, including Beth Tweddle, Louis Smith, Matt Baker and the acrobatic group, Spellbound. These shows have promoted the many benefits attributed to participation in gymnastics.

Louis Smith: Multi-medal winner on pommels at European, world and Olympic competitions and winner of Strictly Come Dancing.

CHAPTER I

AN INTRODUCTION TO GYMNASTICS

Gymnastics has evolved over the years into its present high profile and complex form. There have been a number of significant developments. The progressive changes in the design of gymnastics apparatus has enabled the coaches and gymnasts to increase the

Max Whitlock performs on the rings.

difficulty and complexity of the gymnastic skills.

The sport of gymnastics is controlled ultimately by a world governing body that determines the rules and regulations of the sport. The Fédération Internationale de Gymnastique (FIG) governs the sport at world level and oversees all major gymnastic events, including the Olympic Games, World Championships and Continental championships such as the European, Asian and Pan American Championships.

Each nation has its own national governing body (NGB) and in United Kingdom this is British Gymnastics (BG). BG determines the policies and procedures, and rules and regulations, for the sport in the United Kingdom. The rules are then implemented by the relevant national bodies in England, Wales, Scotland and Northern Ireland. Each of these NGBs is then subdivided into geographical regions to make running the sport much easier at local level.

At the major manifestations such as the Olympic Games, World Championships and European Championships teams and individual gymnasts represent Great Britain, while at other events, such as the Commonwealth Games and other international events, the teams and individuals may represent England, Scotland, Wales or Northern Ireland.

There are many opportunities to participate in gymnastics regardless of ability, age, gender or disability. The sport is very proud of its tradition of catering for all participants through a variety of programmes and there are classes ranging from pre-school, recreational, competitive, and adult or veteran, with disability gymnastics available in all areas.

There are various forms of gymnastics, each with its own apparatus, skills, and rules and regulations. The different types of gymnastics are called disciplines and these include: men's artistic, women's artistic, rhythmic, sports acrobatics, tumbling, free style, trampoline, mini trampoline, recreational, disability and pre-school.

It would be an immense task to do justice to all the disciplines and this publication will focus on men's and women's artistic gymnastics.

The Artistic Gymnastic Disciplines

Women's Artistic Gymnastics (WAG)
This competitive sport is specifically for girls and women. The gymnasts are trained to compete on four pieces of apparatus in the following order:

- Vault
- Uneven bars
- Balance beam
- Floor exercise

Men's Artistic Gymnastics (MAG)
This is restricted to men and boys who train and compete on six pieces of apparatus in the following order:

- Floor exercise
- Side horse/pommel horse
- Still rings
- Vault
- Parallel bars
- Horizontal bar

Competitive Gymnastics

In competitive gymnastics you may take part as an individual or as a member of a team in inter-club competitions, at county or regional level through to national and international events. The events are usually organized on an age or ability basis. The events may be in the form of grades events that consist of compulsory routines and voluntary exercises competitions. The competition structure is based on the age, stage of development and ability of the gymnasts with the demands increasing progressively accordingly. Depending on the stage of development and level of competition, the intensity of training and the number of hours of training will increase gradually to in excess of 30 hours per week. To compete successfully at any level requires a great deal of commitment and dedication, not only from the gymnasts but also from their parents and their coaches.

It is important the coach, gymnast and parents have open and honest discussions about the gymnast's desires, ability, ambitions and true potential before embarking on an intensive competitive training programme and regime.

Coaching Qualifications in Gymnastics

The standard of coaching and coach education of gymnastics at all levels in the United Kingdom is held in high regard throughout the world of sport. British Gymnastics (BG) has been at the forefront of coach education and coach development for many years. It is the

THE STARS OF THE ARTISTIC GYMNASTICS SCENE

Beth Tweddle at the Olympics. She is a multi-gold medal winner at World and European level. Tweddle trained at Park Road Gymnastics Club in Liverpool.

Louis Smith in a flair on the pommel horse. When he won a bronze medal at the Beijing Olympics. He became the first British gymnast to win an Olympic medal for more than 100 years. Smith trains at Huntingdon Gymnastics Club.

Max Whitlock performs a flair. He won an all-around silver medal at the World Championships and became Great Britain's first ever World Champion, winning gold on the pommel horse at the 2015 World Championships. Whitlock is a multi-medal winner at European, World, Olympic and Commonwealth championships. Perhaps our greatest ever gymnast, he trains at South Essex Gym Club.

Claudia Fragapane during her floor routine. She burst on to the senior gymnastic scene when she won four gold medals at the 2014 Commonwealth Games. Fragapane trains at Bristol Hawkes Gym Club.

philosophy of British Gymnastics to develop, implement, monitor and continually evaluate a coach education programme that meets the needs of the coaches and the gymnasts. The syllabus that describes the content of the coach education learning programme has evolved around the changing needs of the sport. The content of the syllabus and the coach education programme provides the knowledge, understanding and means to enable the coach to deliver high quality and safe coaching at the appropriate level.

Qualification Pathway for Gymnastics Coaches

In the past decade the responsibility for overseeing the standardization of coaching qualifications across all sports has been transferred to Sports Coach UK. All coaching qualifications must meet a set of national standards in order to become recognized on the UK Coaching Certificate (UKCC) approved qualifications list.

British Gymnastics is the recognized governing body for gymnastics in the UK. It provides a wide range of options for entry into coaching. The organization has designed a structure of certificated awards and qualifications that are approved by UKCC. This permits anybody with an interest in coaching to enter the process and then progress their knowledge and effectiveness as a coach through a series of qualifications. **Certificated awards** include the Helpers and the Leaders awards.

The **Helper's award** is designed to allow interested parents or young gymnasts, as young as fourteen, to help a qualified coach in such areas as group organization, observing behaviour, helping to lift gymnasts on to the equipment, registration, dispersal and other general tasks.

They are not qualified to coach or take responsibility for any part of the coaching

session but can provide valuable assistance to the coach.

In addition to the tasks undertaken by the Helpers award, the **Leader's award** allows the holder to assist in the delivery of the warm-up and cool down sessions and to support the gymnasts for the physical preparation and conditioning exercises. They may also provide useful help when gymnasts are undergoing physical profile testing or when they are being assessed for the achievement awards.

British Gymnastics Coaching Qualification Pathway

The **coaching qualifications** framework includes qualifications from Level 1 through to Level 6.

Level 1 Assistant Coach (AC)

This permits the AC to assist more qualified coaches to the level of gymnastic skills contained in the AC syllabus. The minimum age for enrolment on to the course is fifteen but no previous experience is needed to register.

Level 2 Coach (C)

This qualifies a coach to take responsibility for a group of gymnasts working to the level of the Level 2 syllabus that contains the main foundation gymnastic skills of level A. The Level 2 coach may supervise Level 1 coaches and those people who possess Helpers or Leaders awards. The prerequisites for entry on to the Level 2 course are a minimum age of eighteen and possession of a Level 1 qualification.

Level 3 Club Coach (CC)

This qualification entitles the CC to operate independently and take responsibility for a club or specific discipline within a club to the skill level as depicted in the Level 3 sylla-

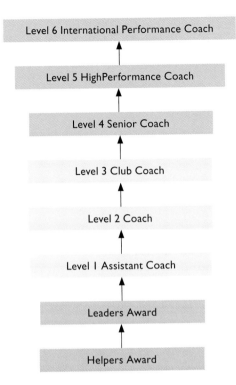

Level 6 International Performance Coach

↑

Level 5 HighPerformance Coach

↑

Level 4 Senior Coach

↑

Level 3 Club Coach

↑

Level 2 Coach

↑

Level I Assistant Coach

↑

Leaders Award

↑

Helpers Award

coaching high performance gymnasts to the level of C and D skills. Their knowledge and understanding of sport science and its application to high performance coaching will be extended. Coaches must have proven experience and ability to coach gymnasts effectively to the level of the Level 4 syllabus.

Level 6 International Performance Coach (IPC)

At this level, entrance on to the training course will be by invitation and is offered to highly skilled and capable coaches who possess a Level 5 qualification. This will enable coaches to teach skills of the highest complexity, including E to F level skills, and Level 6 coaches may develop previously untried gymnastic elements.

The Structure of the Training Courses

British Gymnastics (BG) has a very successful coach education programme that provides the opportunity for coaches to learn and qualify through structured and progressive learning and development. The training courses are supplemented by excellent resource materials and coaching logbooks designed specifically for each level of coaching course. Following attendance on the training course, candidates then follow a post-course development period that involves completing certain tasks with the help of a mentor coach. The assessment process includes a theory and practical coach assessment together with appraisal of the coach's logbook. Support and advice is offered at each point in the coach's personal development by BG and its coach education staff.

Support for Coaches in Gymnastics

British Gymnastics has introduced a coach development fund, which is an opportunity for prospective new and developing coaches

bus. The syllabus includes the basic core gymnastic skills of A and B levels. Entrants for this level must be eighteen and hold a Level 2 coaching qualification in the appropriate discipline.

Level 4 Senior Coach (SC)

This entitles the coach to teach more advanced skills at B and C levels and introduces a more scientific approach to the principles that underpin coaching of gymnastics. This includes such topics as detailed planning, exercise physiology and applied biomechanics. Coaches wishing to enrol for this course must have demonstrated their ability and commitment by involvement in the development of Level 3 standard gymnasts.

Level 5 High Performance Coach (HPC)

Coaches at this level will be instructed on

to apply for funding to attend a recognized coach education course. These funding opportunities allow a 50 per cent reduction on the cost of a Level 1 or Level 2 course and the grants are available in each of the gymnastic disciplines.

This funding is targeted towards priority areas as identified by the BG area managers. Applicants must be members of British Gymnastics, must meet the prerequisites for the particular course and applications should be made via the area managers.

It is also possible to receive coaching grants or sponsorship from other sources, such as the gymnastics clubs or local sports development associations. Try searching your local area gymnastics websites to find further information.

CHAPTER 2

THE BENEFITS OF PARTICIPATING IN SPORTS

The Characteristics Associated with Participation in Sport

There are millions of people participating in amateur and professional sport and they do so for a variety of reasons. These may include to improve their fitness, for social reasons, because they wish to be challenged or so they are able to compete. However, it may be unwise to assume that participation in sport does not have undesirable side effects. As potential coaches we should consider both the good and less good effects of sports participation.

Some Negative Aspects of Sports Participation

It is generally recognized that the majority of children will have a desire to participate in some form of sport. This will require a set of rules that will challenge all the participants and determine how

points or goals are scored. This sounds quite natural but if the rules result in a winner being determined then someone has to be a loser.

Obviously the winner will get the accolade and praise he or she deserves but what effect does this have on children who frequently end up as losers? This would almost certainly affect their self-confidence and could cause them to leave the sport or activity as they

Erika Fasana on the beam.

become unhappy and their desire to participate diminishes.

Yes, we should praise the winner as there is little wrong with being a winner, but if we can also give recognition and praise to the other participants for their skills, hard work and effort, we might motivate them to remain in the sport.

It is interesting to observe the parents of children who are involved in sport. Quite often you will observe the parent who is living life through the skills and success of their children. Such parents are often overzealous and place far too much pressure to succeed upon their children. The effect is that they frequently counter the guidance of the coach, sometimes overloading the children with their own expectations. They frequently offer external rewards for success in an attempt to motivate the child. These often unrealistic targets almost certainly lead to the child 'failing' to meet these targets set by their parents and being disappointed that they did not receive the promised trophies. This in turn leads to the children losing interest and ceasing to enjoy the sport. The combined effect often results in the children dropping out of the sport.

It may be surprising that recent research has confirmed that the majority of children of both sexes prefer to succeed in a sporting environment rather than in an academic field.

Children often seek out competitive situations in order to gain feedback about their physical ability in comparison with their peers and this endorses the fact that the perception of physical ability is a high priority for children.

There is also strong evidence that the importance of being physically able in the eyes of their peers has a high priority in children since they perceive this makes them more readily accepted and therefore will have greater opportunities to develop their social skills.

Children who are less physically able are often 'locked out' of team selection situations and are therefore disadvantaged when trying to establish friendships within peer groups.

Consequently the less physically able children often suffer low self-esteem and self-worth and this leads to feelings of anxiety and stress. Perhaps these are part of the reason why some children grow up learning to dislike sport.

Another concern in sport is the situation where a coach may 'over-train' a young person or exploit their talents merely to demonstrate his or her ability as a coach. In a sport such as gymnastics, where young children are involved, there is a danger of the coach attempting to teach advanced skills without first developing the prerequisite level of physical fitness or without using the required sequence of progressive skills. This is obviously dangerous and may lead to unnecessary injury.

It is also important to remember that children are not young adults and that their young growing bodies can easily be overloaded with excessive training demands that can lead to permanent damage.

The author has deliberately included these undesirable and often detrimental effects of sport to express a genuine concern for the need for potential coaches to strive to avoid or eliminate them.

The Benefits Derived from Participating in Sport

Sport is usually highly valued by children as it plays a key role in their physical and psychological development. Sport participation should be predominately enjoyable, particularly in the early years of the child's development. Sport should offer realistic challenges with opportunities to experience the pleasure of achieving a target or mastering a skill at the desired and appropriate level. For some participants the motivation to play sport is be a 'winner' or to show their superiority of physical skill or strength over others.

However, the main benefits of participation in sport, whether this is for competitive or recreational purposes, are generally recognized as being improvements in physical fitness, social skills, personality, character development, decision making and problem solving and discipline.

The Additional Benefits of Participation in Gymnastics

In addition to the benefits generally associated with involvement in sport, a child practising any gymnastic discipline will undoubtedly attain increased benefits through:

Flexibility
From an early age the children will gain improved range of movement in the various joint complexes through involvement in a controlled programme of progressive stretching exercises. This improvement in flexibility will improve the ability to learn the gymnastic skills and may also reduce the risk of injury.

Strength
Generally a gymnast is considered to be one of the strongest and fittest of all athletes. The remarkable degree of strength is developed over many years through a carefully structured programme of strength training using the body's own weight as the resistance load.

Balance
Participation in gymnastics will ensure the child is able to understand fully the various body shapes and how to adjust the position of their centre of mass (c of m) above their support point in order to maintain their balance.

Co-ordination
Gymnastics will enable a child to develop safely and progressively the fundamental skills including crawling, walking and running, and the more advanced foundation skills such as springing, jumping, twisting and landing. The child will learn how to co-ordinate the limbs of the body to enable these basic functions to be done correctly and efficiently. This basic movement vocabulary is the foundation upon which the more complex movement patterns are based.

Spatial Awareness
This is the ability to understand what shape your body is making and where your body is in flight in relation to the ground. It is an important characteristic that is developed to a high degree through the performance of the many varied gymnastic skills.

Standards of Behaviour
Injuries are an inherent risk in all sports but these risks can be greatly reduced by safe practice and the avoidance of horseplay. In the complex sport of gymnastics, the risks can be reduced not only by good physical preparation and progressive skills but by the use of controlled discipline and appropriate behaviour. This does not require a regimented, controlled regime but does need good standards of behaviour to avoid unnecessary collisions or mishaps, which may be caused by misbehaviour.

Alertness and Concentration
Gymnastic activities will enhance the psychological abilities of the child by training the child to visualize movement patterns mentally, make quick and appropriate decisions on what movements to deploy, react immedi-

ately to situations and to focus readily attention on the matter in hand.

Academic Achievement

There has been over the years many anecdotal instances of gymnasts exceeding their predicted level of academic achievements. This is thought to be attributable to their greater ability to concentrate, increased discipline and their ability to organize their study time and gymnastics training schedule into their normal lifestyle. Academic achievements may also be enhanced through the greater self-confidence and self-belief derived through participation in gymnastic activities.

Ability to Fall Safely

Gymnasts are taught how to fall correctly and how to safely abort a movement to reduce the risk of injury. These reactions will be adopted almost automatically once they have been learned and reduce the fear of falling greatly.

Bone Density

There is a great deal of evidence to show that participation in sporting activities increases the bone density of growing children. This results in the bone being less likely to break due to excessive twisting or impact. In gymnastic activities the loads placed upon the body in order to improve strength are not excessive and are increased progressively. This is a factor that allows the bones to build up their resistance to the loading and become more dense. There are fewer incidents of collisions and bone breakages in gymnastics than most sports.

CHAPTER 3

THE ROLE OF THE COACH

A coach of young people will have many roles to fulfil. He or she must be fully aware of the effect these roles will have on the overall well-being and development of the young people. The list of roles is huge but the main ones will undoubtedly involve a young coach becoming all of the following.

Role Model

Your gymnasts will look to you to set standards of behaviour and to lay down appropriate

rules, which must apply equally to all coaches and gymnasts without exception. The young gymnasts in your care will tend to mimic your standard of dress, cleanliness, enthusiasm, punctuality, manner and behaviour.

Teacher

You will need to be a teacher, imparting knowledge and understanding to the gymnasts in your care. This will facilitate the development of the skills needed to enable them to learn new skills and to train safely.

Trainer

This involves introducing physical preparation exercises to enable the gymnasts to develop appropriate levels of fitness in order for them to train and learn safely.

Psychologist

This involves introducing strategies to enable the young gymnasts to visualize their performance, feel the movement and develop confidence and self-esteem. You will teach the gymnasts how to develop coping strategies

British Team Captain Kristian Thomas on rings.

in order to overcome or deal with various psychological scenarios, such as self-doubt, fear and competition nervousness.

Motivator

You need to be able to inspire the gymnasts to set appropriate targets or goals and to encourage them to become self-motivated to strive to achieve those targets.

Disciplinarian

You need to encourage the gymnasts to behave in a manner according to the standards expected of a gymnast and implementing these standards without losing the enjoyment of taking part.

Manager

The coach must be good at planning, organizing, implementing, monitoring, evaluating and reviewing the training programmes. He or she must maintain registers and keep training records and accident reports up to date. They should advise and help the gymnasts to manage their time and lifestyle in order to be able to participate in gymnastics alongside their academic education and other daily demands on their time.

Friend

The coach and gymnasts will form a close partnership over time but this must be an appropriate relationship that should be based upon mutual trust and respect for each other. The coach may also become a confidante to the gymnast and may need to provide support as

their charge passes through the various stages of maturation.

Philosopher

A good coach will form an appropriate coaching philosophy founded upon what motivates them to coach, their commitment to coaching and their personal beliefs.

Reflector

In order to measure the effectiveness of their coaching it is recommended that a coach should frequently reflect upon the degree of success of the training programme and on his or her personal performance as a coach.

The Responsibilities of a Coach

The safety and well-being of the participants is paramount and all coaches owe a duty of care to their athletes. There are both legal and moral responsibilities with which a coach should comply. Some of these responsibilities and the guidelines or policies that affect these responsibilities are described below:

Coaching Code of Ethics
British Gymnastics (BG) has produced a coach's code of practice that details the standard of behaviour expected by all coaches operating under the BG name. This code has been adapted from the one prescribed by Sports Coach UK that must be adhered to by all sports.

This code encompasses the coaches' code of conduct and the coaching code of ethics, and all coaches must always abide by them.

Code of Conduct for Coaches

This states that all coaches must:

- Be trained and qualified to the level of gymnastics they wish to coach
- Provide a safe environment at all times
- Follow recommended coaching practice for coaching each skill
- Ensure the health and welfare of the gymnasts at all times
- Keep their knowledge up to date
- Continually demonstrate their enthusiasm and commitment to coaching
- Dress and behave in a manner expected of a qualified gymnastics coach.

Code of Ethics for Coaching

Coaches have a moral and legal responsibility for their gymnasts with regard to safety, well-being and protection, and the code of ethics details these requirements:

- *Duty of care:* Coaches owe a duty of care towards their gymnasts and must place their safety and well-being as the main priority.
- *Safety and welfare:* Coaches must adhere to the safeguarding children policy for their sport to ensure the participants are not put at risk. If a coach follows the good coaching practice guidelines described in this text, the gymnasts will remain safe and the coach will not be at risk of allegations of poor practice or abuse being made. It is highly recommended that all coaches attend a recognized safeguarding children in sport training course so they can conform to the good practice guidelines.
- *Creating positive relationships:* As a coach you will no doubt form a close relationship with your gymnasts. This relationship must be appropriate and be based on mutual respect and trust. You will be in a position of power with regard to the relationship with your gymnasts and you must not abuse this relationship of trust or your position as a coach.

Equality Code

All participants in gymnastics including gymnasts, coaches and officials must be treated fairly regardless of their gender, sexual orientation, age, parental or marital status, disability, religion, colour, race, ethnic or national origins, or socio/economic background. Discrimination on any grounds should not be tolerated in sport. Gymnastics has a proud record in treating all participants equally and fairly and has done a great deal to ensure that people of all abilities and people with disabilities are integrated fully in the sport.

The Skills Required by a Coach

To be an effective coach you need to be able to multi-task and the skills you will require will include:

Communication: Being able to explain clearly and succinctly what you wish your gymnasts to do in language that they understand is an essential skill of a coach.

Demonstration: You will need to able to present a visual demonstration of the task that you wish your gymnasts to perform. This does not necessarily require you to perform the task personally, but it may be through the use of a visual aid such as a demonstration by a gymnast, a picture, an illustration or DVD. This visual aid will provide your gymnasts with a great deal of valuable information and will enable them to perform or learn the movement.

Teach: To be a successful coach you must be able to adapt and apply the many skills that teaching involves, such as creating a suitable learning environment that encourages and facilitates learning.

Planning: The ability to plan, implement, monitor, analyze, evaluate and review the training programme or lesson is a very important part in the life of a coach. The training plan will become increasingly import as the gymnast progresses and will involve short, medium and long term planning of the training programme and competition schedule.

Observation and analysis: To be a successful coach you must be able to:

- Observe the performance of your gymnast
- Analyze this performance and compare it with the visual model you were expecting to see
- Determine what areas were different and need to be improved
- Identify the corrections that need to be made and determine what action to take.

Motivation: The ability to inspire or motivate your gymnasts will be a constant challenge and is a competence that often defines a successful coach.

Organization, administration and management: It is perhaps every coach's dream to have somebody to take on these important roles. However, in these current times most coaching situations require the coach to be involved in one or more of these skills. This could be through class registrations, planning sessions, completing reports, managing other staff and similarly onerous but important tasks.

The Qualities Possessed by a Good Coach

It is not clear whether good coaches have a natural gift for coaching but what is certain is that they will possess a great passion for it and an enthusiasm for learning all they can to improve. The essential qualities displayed by good and effective coaches include:

A propensity for coaching: It is certain that good coaches have this and maintain an inbuilt desire to help their gymnasts to attain their optimum or desired level of achievement. However, it is very important to remember the gymnasts' desires, needs, ability and level of commitment, together with their safety and well-being, are at the forefront of the 'gymnast-centred coaching process'. It is highly dangerous for a coach to exploit the talents of a gymnast merely to demonstrate his or her ability to coach and to satisfy his or her ego at the expense of the gymnast.

Trained and qualified: Good coaches will ensure they are trained and qualified in the area and to the level they are coaching. Coaches will follow recommended coaching practice and adhere to the codes of practice and coaching standards. As experience is gained, the coach will be encouraged to 'think outside the box' to develop new and interesting techniques to help the gymnast develop and retain interest. These new ideas must be safe and purposeful and should be approved by a more qualified coach before implementation.

Knowledge and understanding: A good coach must be willing to keep up to date with developments in the sport and also in the relevant sport sciences. The coach should study to improve his or her understanding of these subject areas and also develop their ability to apply this knowledge and understanding to enhance effectiveness.

Enthusiasm, reliability and commitment: It is important that a coach can continually demonstrate his or her enthusiasm and love for the sport as well as being able to show dedication and commitment. The gymnasts need to know that if you say you will do something then it is guaranteed it will be done.

Careful training planning: A carefully planned training programme will ensure everything included in the programme will be directed towards the desired outcome without pointless and unnecessary diversions that waste time. A good coach will assess the strengths and weaknesses of his or her individual gymnasts and design a programme of training that meets their individual needs. The process of planning will be covered in more detail later.

Patience: It takes around ten to twelve years to produce a top class gymnast. As a coach of young people you will be involved in many important stages of the gymnast's development, regardless of the final level of attainment. It is very important when teaching a new skill, combination of linked skills or routine to allow time for the gymnast to consolidate each element before progressing. Even though the skill may have been learned or mastered there will almost certainly be a drop in performance each time there is a change in circumstances. The phrase 'patience is a virtue' is certainly true in the profile of an effective and successful coach.

Approachable, honest and trustworthy: It is important that if your gymnasts have a problem they know they can confide in you and that they can trust you to be honest in your actions or advice. They must know you are reliable and that, if necessary and appropriate, the matter will remain confidential.

Prudence and caring: A prudent and caring coach is one who puts the needs and safety of his or her gymnast as the highest priority. This gymnast-centred approach will ensure his or her needs are first and foremost and that recommended practices are followed. Unnecessary risks will be avoided. The good coach will be approachable and will listen to the opinions of others and, in particular, the views of the gymnasts.

Punctuality and professionalism: The coach must set high personal standards and behave in a professional manner at all times. Arrival on time and ensuring that his or her behaviour is impeccable at all times are important qualities.

Empowering the gymnasts: A long term goal of a coach should be to make the gymnast self-sufficient. This will require developing the gymnast as a whole person and to empower him or her to make decisions about training. This can be achieved by frequently asking the gymnast about his or her own performance, what could be done to improve it and discussing personal goals or aims.

Self-appraisal and self-reflection: A very import quality of a coach is the ability to reflect upon your own performance. This will require coaches to analyze their methods and style, and to determine what did and did not work. They will constantly ask the question: 'How could I improve my coaching?' They will focus purposely on the identified area for improvement. It is also very important to ask the gymnasts if your coaching style suits them and to discuss how you could change this to be more effective.

Coaching Philosophy

The over-arching aim of all coaches should be to make participation in sport enjoyable and beneficial, regardless of whether it is competitive or recreational in nature. This should be achieved through the provision of a happy and safe environment in which the young people participate.

With young people the focus on achievement should be directed to the 'mastery of a skill' concept rather than a focus that is based on a 'competitive' orientated goal.

As a coach you are advised strongly to consider your personal values and beliefs relating to sport and your coaching. These should form your values statement and motives for coaching. These will manifest into your **philosophy on coaching**.

As a potential coach it is important to ask yourself the following questions:

Why Do I Want to Coach?

Your possible answers might include: I like working with children; I get a kick out of seeing someone achieve something I have helped to coach; I am good at communicating information to children; I have a good rapport with youngsters; the children seem to respond to me; I am able to motivate young people; or I want to stay in sport or be involved in sport. All these reasons are acceptable but I doubt whether anyone gave a reason for coaching as 'coaching satisfies my own needs'. This is an important factor since I doubt that you will continue coaching if your own ego and your personal needs are not being satisfied.

What Do I Want to Achieve Through my Coaching?

Your responses may include one or more of the following: I want to help children enjoy their sport; I want to give children the opportunities that I had; I want to help the children achieve their optimum level of achievement; I want to help the sport grow or achieve greater success; I want to pass on my knowledge and skills on to others; I want to produce a champion; I want to work with motivated children who want to reach their optimal level of performance; or I want to be recognized by my peers as a successful coach. All of these are commendable reasons for wanting to coach.

How Will I Cope with Failure?

You may consider that failure will drive you to become more determined to succeed in the future. This is very commendable and you may believe this shows strength of character and commitment to your goals, but ask yourself the question: 'Is failure the same as losing?'

It is possible to lose a match or not win a medal even though the children you are coaching may have produced their best performance. It may have been unrealistic to expect your gymnasts to win or come first but if you had set a different goal, say 'to perform without a major fall' then they may well have achieved this challenge and everybody could be delighted. Their motivation could be enhanced. The saying 'winning isn't everything' can be used in to good effect if you set the appropriate goals or targets.

How will you react to the case where your gymnasts did not perform to your or their expectations? Do you show your disappointment visually and verbally and immediately chastise them for underperforming or do you blame anyone but yourself? Hopefully none of these will be your reaction. You will learn to initially offer praise for the effort shown by your gymnasts and tell them you will discuss the outcome at some future time. This shows your support for your gymnasts and then gives you time to analyze and reflect on the performance and formulate how you will address the situation.

What is your Opinion on Cheating?

You may believe in fair play but would your resolve be tested if it meant that you could lose an event or competition by sticking to your beliefs?

What is your reaction to cheating or bending the rules to gain an unfair advantage? Are you honest, trusting, accepting and forgiving? These are moral factors that will be tested in your role as a coach and should form part of your beliefs and coaching philosophy.

Remember, as a coach the children may look at you in awe and see you as a strong role model. You need to be confident in your coaching philosophy and discuss this with your young gymnasts, their parents and other coaches so your beliefs and intentions are clear.

How are you on Making and Keeping Promises?

As a coach you will at some stage be setting behavioural standards that must apply to everybody from the coach, assistant coaches, the more senior gymnasts and new beginners without exception. If you cannot practise what you preach you will be breaking your trust with your gymnasts and may lose their respect.

Remember, honesty is the best approach. Don't promise that you will make a child into a champion if you don't have the knowledge, skills, commitment, dedication or the facility this will ultimately require.

KEY POINTS FOR BECOMING A SUCCESSFUL COACH

- Be aware of your roles and responsibilities
- Behave in a professional manner
- Be honest, trustworthy, reliable and approachable
- Be reflective; identify your own strengths and weaknesses and build on your strengths while striving to make your weaknesses into strengths
- Formulate your coaching philosophy based upon your beliefs
- Discuss your philosophy with your colleagues and gymnasts
- Occasionally review the reasons why you coach to ensure they remain the right ones.

CHAPTER 4

THE PRINCIPLES OF LEARNING

Aliya Mustafina executes a turn on the asymetric bars.

There are many factors that will influence the process of learning and we will commence this fascinating section with the stages of development that all children will undergo.

The Stages of Child Development

Gymnastics is a sport for people of all abilities and all ages. It caters for young children under six years of age, through the pre-pubertal and post-pubertal periods of growth right through to adulthood. It is important to remember that children are not mini adults and not machines and must therefore be treated according to their differing needs.

We, as coaches of young people, must have a sound understanding of how a child grows and develops, both physically and psychologically. We will therefore look at a simple overview of the important factors in the growth and development in children.

Age and Stage of Maturation of the Developing Child

You may have noticed how children of the same chronological age possess different abilities. Some may be bigger, stronger and have developed a greater vocabulary of words and movement skills than other children of similar age.

Children all pass through the same stages of development but they do so at different rates. It is not until the post-pubertal stage of development that the growth patterns will be completed.

It is important for a coach to appreciate the abilities a child possesses at each stage of maturation and which types of skill or challenges are best taught at each stage of development. It is important to note that the ages stated in the following text are approximate since these may be affected by the different rates of development and the fact that females tend to develop more rapidly than their male counterparts in the earlier stages.

Early Childhood (up to Six Years)

At this stage the children are concerned with learning the 'fundamental movement skills' such as crawling, walking, running, hopping, skipping, springing, jumping, landing and rolling. These are some of the skills that should be taught at this early stage of development.

The child's aerobic fitness is good so they are very active. They possess relatively good grip strength and this invariably exceeds their support strength. Mentally their concentration levels are not good and consequently the session needs to be limited to 30 to 40 minutes and the activities should be many and varied. The sessions should be safe, interesting and challenging but most of all they must be fun and enjoyable.

Late Childhood (Six to Eight Years)

During this stage of development we need to concentrate on developing such skills as movement co-ordination, 'foundation movement skills' and core gymnastic skills. General physical preparation (sometimes referred to as conditioning) should commence and this should include mid-body control exercises (core strength), light passive flexibility training and exercise using the gymnast's own body weight to improve general strength.

It is recommended that the training times should be between 4 and 6 hours per week at this stage of maturation.

Pre-Pubertal Stage of Development (Eight to Ten Years)

The potential for developing speed and mobility is high at this stage and the ability to learn a range of basic gymnastic skills is also very good. The young bodies are amenable to improvements in flexibility and to improved all-round strength and fitness.

Concentration levels will be much improved and basic technical skills can be taught and refined. It is recommended that the training hours can be increased safely up to 10 hours per week.

Early Pubertal Stage of Development (Ten to Thirteen Years)

This is the stage where the child will experience rapid growth spurts. Coaches must be constantly observant to the onset of a growth spurt since during this period the bones grow rapidly and the length and strength of the muscles will lag behind. Consequently the range of movement may be reduced temporarily, co-ordination will suffer and previously learned skills may become erratic as a result. Hence the emphasis on training should be on regaining the flexibility and strength together with improving and perfecting the previously learned core skills. During this period of growth the gymnasts may become frustrated at their perceived lack of improvement and it is important that a coach can explain the cause of this frustration. The programme can be varied to include experimenting with new skills to retain the gymnast's interest and focus.

Late Pubertal Stage of Development (Thirteen to Fifteen Years)

At this stage the rate of growth usually tapers off and the capacity to gain strength increases. The emphasis should be on strength training that can be more specific to the gymnast's needs and the skills he or she is about to learn. The improvements in strength means that more advanced skills can be learned and mastered.

Training times can be increased to fifteen hours per week. The hormonal changes within the body during this stage of growth can lead to extreme changes in character and mood swings but thankfully these are usually only temporary. Patience is a good virtue for coaches to possess during this period when teenagers enter a period where they believe they know better than everyone else what is best for them.

Post-Pubertal Stage of Maturation (Fifteen Years+)

Usually the body will continue to grow until the ages of eighteen in the case of girls and nineteen in males but the changes are much finer during this progression towards full maturation.

Retention of flexibility together with more specific strength exercises are a priority and the level of complexity of skills and routines can be increased in line with the increases in strength and fitness.

Key Points

- Always be aware of the changes that occur during each of the stages of maturation and growth and adapt the training accordingly
- Be particularly alert to the onset of growth spurts during the stages of puberty since the potential for frustration and injury is at its greatest during this period of development

- The pre-pubertal stage is perhaps the best period to improve flexibility.

How Skills are Learned

There are many theories on how people learn and how best to teach them or help them. Before we consider how we can help people to learn we need to look at the principles of learning.

For learning to take place the learner must be:

- Motivated to want to learn
- Prepared to repeat or practise that which is to be learned
- Given feedback to inform them how well they are doing.

The Stages of Learning

When we strive to learn something the process will pass through three stages. Consider a situation where a gymnast is faced with learning a new practical skill with which you are familiar.

Firstly, the cognitive stage: The first stage of learning is commensurate with trying to sort out which movements are required to be produced, in which order and how forcefully or rapidly they need to be done. The learner is attempting get some mental understanding and feeling for the new movement pattern. The performances will be erratic, lack efficiency and, at first, will be awkward and not smooth. The performer will require constant feedback to help him or her to work out what is correct and what is not.

Secondly, the associative stage: During this stage of learning the performance errors are less erratic and the movements will become more consistent. The gymnast is forming a better understanding of the desired movement pattern but will still require some less frequent and subtle feedback.

Thirdly, the autonomous stage: The gymnast will be able to perform the skill without much conscious thought of the mechanics and will be aware of any errors in performance. The skill is said to have become 'over learned'. The skill will be performed consistently and almost automatically. The gymnast will require only intermittent or irregular feedback as he or she makes subtle adjustments to master and consolidate the technique.

Methods of Learning

As well as going through the various stages of learning, the learner may have a preferred style such as visual (seeing), auditory (hearing) and kinaesthetic (feeling).

Visual learning is where the learner gathers information by observing a performance or viewing a picture or illustration. Through these visual aids the learner can gather a great deal of information about the required movement pattern, height and speed. It is often said that a picture speaks a thousand words, which is perhaps true if you have a visual style of preferred learning.

Auditory learning, or verbal learning, is achieved through listening, writing and reading. This is perhaps favoured by people who are experienced, but can you be sure that the learner has correctly understood what was said? Auditory learning for novice participants may not be so successful on its own.

Table 1   The Style of Learning and the Method of Coaching.

Method of Learning	Style of Coaching	Typical example
Visual	Demonstration	Watching another gymnast perform the skill
Auditory or verbal	Instruction or explanation	Instructing (telling) the gymnast what to do
Kinaesthetic	Physical or manual	Physically shaping the gymnast through the skill feeling the skill

Kinaesthetic learning is where the pupil learns by physically doing something. They learn through the understanding the muscle movement required to produce the skill and also through the sensations experienced in performing the skill.

Different people have different preferred learning styles and it is recommended that we use a range of them to maximize potential and ensure that everybody's needs are met.

Research has identified that children between nine and eleven years of age are most likely to adopt a 'mastery of skill' perspective to their learning style and goal setting. Thus when given a new skill to learn, the main focus is on learning or mastery of the skill to the best of their ability. However, between the ages of eleven to twelve the emphasis changes to a more competitive focus where the children are concerned with demonstrating their ability compared with the ability of their peers. This concept of perceived high physical ability and comparison with peers is ego driven. If the child's ego is not constantly being satisfied by winning frequently or being successful then he or she may withdraw from sport.

Boys are generally thought to have more of a competitive goal perspective than girls.

Key Points

- It is often more effective to use at least two styles of coaching together in order to ensure that the information is clear. Using a demonstration or manual style accompanied by verbal key points is combining two methods of learning and is understood more readily

- Ask yourself: How do I know for certain that the learner has correctly understood?

- It is good coaching practice to question the gymnast after the instruction. Try asking: 'What do you need to focus on?' Follow this up with asking: 'Why is that?' or 'What effect will that produce?' These or similar questions are designed to ascertain that the gymnast has understood your feedback correctly.

CHAPTER 5

HOW TO COACH

The Principles of Coaching

The Coaching Process

You may often hear coaches refer to the coaching process as being the Plan – Do – Review process, but it is in fact more complex than that. The process actually forms a loop comprising of a number of key factors, as shown in the diagram below.

The coaching process commences with the **plan** where the coach sets out in detail the planned content of the session or coaching programme.

The coach then **organizes** the gymnastic facilities, the apparatus, equipment, training aids and perhaps other coaches for the delivery of the session.

The session is then **implemented** (delivered) and the coach **monitors** (observes and records) what happened during it. Then by **evaluating** the 'what worked well' and 'what didn't work so well' aspects of the session and identifying how it could be improved, the appropriate sections can be **reviewed** and amended. The new amended plan is then implemented and the loop begins again.

Dan Keatings performs an Endo circle on the horizontal bar.

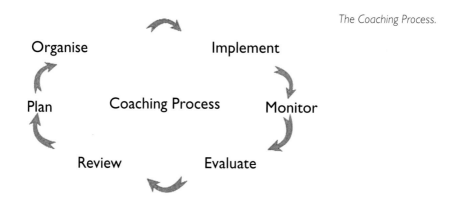

The Coaching Process.

How to Coach

We have looked at how people learn and the coaching process loop. In this section we will look at the concept of **how to coach** and later we will consider **what to coach**.

Many of us will have experienced the most widely used **show and tell** style of coaching. This is where the coach shows a demonstration of the skill or manoeuvre to be learned and provides instructions on the key points he or she wants his gymnasts to focus on in order to learn the new task.

This coaching method has two good qualities. The demonstration is visual and the instruction is verbal and together this caters for two styles of learning, **visual** and **auditory**. If we then added the **kinaesthetic** style by allowing the physical practice of the task a third method of learning has been added. This will enhance the possibilities of more gymnasts being able to learn the skill successfully. This has been proven to be an effective coaching style but more recently another style has been promoted. In this style the coach frequently 'asks questions' to tease out from the gymnasts themselves what they need to do to progress, This might include the next progression or part skill for correcting errors in performance. This **question and answer** method can be a slow process but when used in conjunction with the other styles of coaching it can be very useful in helping the students think with more focused attention about what they need to do to improve.

The question and answer style requires the coach to pose open ended questions to the gymnasts such as:

- How did that attempt compare with the previous one?
- When did you feel your legs bend?
- What do you think you need to do to improve?
- Which part of the skill could we practice to make progress?

The questions should frequently follow the coach commenting initially on the gymnast's effort, not just the quality of the performance. Try using: 'Good effort, now what do we need to concentrate on to improve the performance.' If you don't get the response you expected, follow the initial question with a follow-up question to evoke the correct response. This method of question and answer may take some time to become familiar with but it will help your gymnasts learn and will confirm their level of understanding of the movement pattern they are attempting.

The questions described above are called open questions as they require the recipient to provide more than a one word answer. You are advised to avoid using closed questions such as: 'Can you feel your legs bend?' or 'Do you understand?' as these can be answered with 'yes' or 'no' responses and provide you with little information regarding the real level of the gymnast's understanding.

Remember it is also good practice to complete the feedback loop by asking your gymnast, just before their next attempt: 'What did we decide we were going to focus on?' and follow this with: 'Why, or what effect will that have?' or similar questions. This will enable you to check that the gymnast has understood the feedback and will ensure he or she concentrates on the key factor just prior to the next attempt.

Using this technique will enhance your coaching since the gymnast's mind will be more focused.

Providing Feedback

The feedback loop shows the key factors involved in the 'how to coach' model, so let us explore the content more fully. The coaching starts with a set of skills the coach wants the gymnast to learn and these will be introduced by a visual illustration or demonstration accompanied by suitable instruction and key points.

The tasks are then performed by the gymnast and the performance is observed by the coach. The coach will create a mental image of the performance and with practice will be able to recall the performance, rather like replaying a video or CD. The performance will then be analyzed by comparing the actual performance to a model of a competent or desired performance in order to identify similarities and differences between them.

The coach should then pick out the key good points and identify the areas requiring attention.

At this point many coaches provide their feedback to the gymnast but they will be missing a valuable part of the learning process if they do so. It is far more beneficial to ask the gymnast to comment on his or her (or perhaps a peer's performance) prior to offering feedback. Ask the gymnast: 'How would you describe the performance? Was it better, worse, higher, lower, faster or slower than the required level or the previous attempt?'

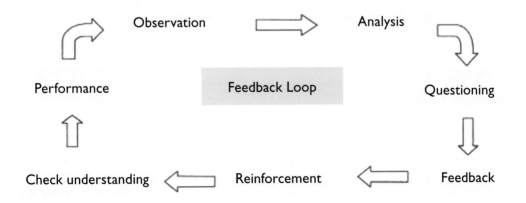

The feedback loop.

Perhaps at a later stage in the learning of a skill ask the gymnast: 'What shape was your body in,' or: 'At what point did you feel your legs bend,' or similar questions. This will encourage the gymnast to think about the performance and will help the coach to gauge whether or not the gymnast understands or feels the required movement pattern in order to perform the skill successfully. If he or she gives you the answers you were expecting then they are on a good learning pathway.

A good coach will then give themselves a few seconds of thinking time to decide what key points to give as feedback. The author has observed coaches frequently giving feedback almost before the gymnast has completed the performance. This is pointless since the gymnast will most likely still be in performance mode rather than being able to listen to any comments directed towards them. So before giving your feedback it is recommended that you adopt the following process:

- **Analyze** the performance
- **Compare** the performance with a good model
- **Identify** the key good points and areas requiring attention
- **Allow time** for the gymnast to come out of performance mode
- **Question** the gymnast about the performance
- **Give yourself time** to gather your thoughts and decide on the most important key points before you provide your feedback.

When providing your feedback to the gymnast it is recommended that you adopt the sequence:

- **Commence** with some positive points such as: 'Great effort or this particular part was good'

- **Give some technical advice** or one or two key points on how the performance can be improved
- **Followed by a positive comment**

This is usually referred to as the 'feedback sandwich'.

Effective Communication Styles

Communication is the means through which meaningful information is shared with others. To be an effective coach you will need to be able to establish effective communication with your gymnast in a manner he or she understands. It should be a two-way process where you are both able to express yourselves but it is also essential that you are both effective at listening to what is being communicated and able to respond appropriately.

Verbal Communication

This is perhaps the most simple form of communication and in a coaching environment it would involve the coach talking to or instructing the gymnast while he or she listens to your words and responds according to your instructions. They should be allowed to ask questions for clarification and you should respond to answer their question. What you say and how you say it is very important so it must be clear and succinct. Remember that people may interpret what you say differently so it is important to check their understanding by questioning them.

Communication is not that simple as verbal communication on its own is almost impossible. It is usually accompanied by some form of body expression or non-verbal communication. Good communicators will often use hand gestures or body movements as they speak in order to bring interest or greater effect to their communication style.

It is not just what you say but how you say it and how your body movements express your

Key Points on Verbal Communication

- Level of language and choice of words
- Tone of voice
- Expression or emphasis on words
- Length of descrptions

Key Points on Non-Verbal Communication

- Remember to:
- Mantain eye contact
- Smile
- Nod in agreement
- Keep a non-threatening body posture

Do not:
- Frown or contort your facial expression
- Sigh
- Tap your feet
- Fold your arms showing your resistance to what is being said

Verbal and non-verbal communication.

intent. Each individual will develop his or her own style of communication and it is important to remember the key points.

As a coach you will become aware of the preferred type of communication for each individual gymnast and how this might change with a mood swing. Once you have given some verbal instructions it is important to question the gymnast to check he or she has interpreted and understood what you have said. It is also important to allow time for the individual to think and respond to your question and also remember to show you are listening to what they are saying.

Coaching Styles

As a coach you may be required to coach individuals of all abilities and ages with varying levels of experience. Your aim should be to help each gymnast achieve his or her personal goals and to enable him or her to perform to their optimum or appropriate level. The individual goals may range from someone simply wanting to enjoy themself through to achieving a high level of performance. You must therefore be able to plan appropriate lessons or sessions and be able to change the manner through which you approach your coaching to suit the needs of the different demands and

Demonstration Explanation	Question and Answer	Organization and Planning
Key Points and Feedback	Safety and Wellbeing	Reinforcement Focus Attention
Gymnastics Knowledge	Checking Understanding	Observation and Analysis

The essential qualities of a good coach.

needs of the individual. It is quite normal to adopt a strict manner with potentially disruptive children but then relax your manner when the children listen and apply themselves to the tasks you have set them. These different coaching approaches are called coaching styles and the range and attributes of each style are described below.

In 1986 two educationalists, Mosston and Ashworth, produced a classification system they called the spectrum of teaching styles, which was based upon their observations and research into physical education. This resulted in a theory that teaching and learning are based upon decision making related to 'what to teach', 'when to teach' and 'how to teach or present the skills' to enable pupils to learn. This was then translated into a continuum in which at one end the teacher makes all the decisions of what, when and how while at the other end of the spectrum the pupils are empowered to make their own decisions.

Clearly we can translate this theory to coaching. From this continuum Mosston and Ashworth devolved ten styles of teaching, of which four are directly relevant to coaching.

Command Style

This is at the teacher-centred end of the continuum and involves the teacher making all the decisions and controlling the activities or tasks and the rate of progress. This style is used when the teacher requires good control over what the learner is doing and is particularly helpful when working with an inexperienced pupil. Detailed command style instruction may be useful in communicating technical instruction but the danger is the pupil will become over-reliant on the teacher (coach) since the pupil will have little opportunity to explore, make decisions and think for himself.

Practice Style or (Task Style)

This style of teaching involves the use of pre-prepared instruction or task cards with instructions, illustrations, techniques and suggested practices to describe a series of learning and practice tasks. This approach provides the learner with the resources but allows the pupil to learn at his or her own pace. This is particularly useful for learners of different abilities and enables the pupil to make some decisions and to remove some of the reliance on the teacher. This style may be used with a group of gymnasts who have different abilities or where they are progressing at different rates and where different challenges can be safely set for each individual. However, this style may increase the level of risk and may become difficult to manage in a gymnastic environment.

Guided Discovery Style

In this style of teaching the learners may be given a broad challenge and the task is

Teacher (Coach) Centred   Pupil (Gymnast) Centred

The Teacher (or Coach) makes all the decisions on what, when and how to teach the skills

The pupils (Gymnasts) are involved in making the decisions about their learning

The teacher–pupil continuum.

to find a way of achieving the task without initial instruction on a technique from the teacher. For instance the teacher (coach) may ask the pupil to perform a cartwheel with a quarter turn. This may result in a number of responses, which may include leading with the left or right leg; placing the hands as for a handstand, or perhaps placing the hands in line in succession; bringing the legs together or keeping them separate; or making a quarter to inwards or outwards. The pupils would develop the ability to listen to and interpret instructions and would learn to find solutions to problems and discover what works for them. However, this can be time consuming, requires frequent feedback and may lead to poor or inaccurate technique being learned.

Discovery Style

At the other end of the spectrum of teaching styles is the pupil-centred discovery style of learning. Here the pupils learn to discover solutions and responses to tasks or problems. This enables them to identify the problem or task and make decisions through a variety of possible solutions to discover what is the most appropriate response. Using the discovery style with young inexperienced pupils in gymnastics could be dangerous and may lead to them learning poor techniques and bad habits. However, at a later stage of their development this style will enable the coach to empower the gymnasts to become self-sufficient and not totally dependent on the coach.

Clearly we can apply these teaching theories to produce a continuum of coaching styles but we will add a further dimension to the spectrum of coaching styles.

Types of Coach

The manner in which you deliver your style of coaching will have an influence on how you are perceived and how effective you

become. The various demeanours portrayed by coaches include:

The Authoritarian Coach

This coach is often fanatical about his/her sport, is usually well organized, plans the training carefully, expects obedience, demands attention to detail, makes all the decisions and expects results. The disciplined environment this approach creates is often conducive to success providing that the gymnasts are of suitably strong character and motivated towards achievement. However, this approach may not suit introverted or more sensitive characters.

The Casual Coach

This coach is easy going and will produce a relaxed atmosphere in the gym. This type of coach does not spend a great deal of time planning the training and is often ill prepared. The training will be on a spur of the moment basis and great success in performance is unlikely. However, the gymnasts by default may become self-sufficient and not totally dependent on the coach.

The Nice Guy Coach

This manner of coaching portrays the coach as being pleasant, creative, concerned about the well-being of the gymnasts and flexible in regard to the training regime. This usually creates a relaxed and enjoyable training environment in which success is enjoyed and failure is not seen as being a real irreparable problem. This coach is often open to manipulation by those gymnasts with strong characters since he or she may be too willing to listen to suggestions for changes or adaptations.

The Autocratic Coach

This coaching manner is similar to the authoritarian coach in that they will be well organized, the training will be planned in detail and the coach will make all the decisions. He or she will provide frequent instructions to the gymnasts in an adult-to-child type of communication on how they want the skills or tasks performed. They will provide feedback based entirely on their observations and experience without any input from the gymnasts. The atmosphere in the gymnasium will be more relaxed but the coach is the font of all knowledge.

The Democratic Coach

In this environment the coach relates to the performers in an adult-to-adult manner and invites the gymnast to have an input into planning the training, decision-making and observations on performances. He or she will consult the gymnast, asking for his or her opinions before making a joint decision. This allows more involvement in decision-making by the gymnast regarding training and this helps his or her motivation to achieve a goal due to increased feelings of owner-ship of the session. This enhances the ability to recognize problems, identify suitable solutions and improves decision-making ability. This encourages self-sufficiency in the gymnast and reduces the level of depen-dency on the coach. However, this movement towards a totally democratic manner of coaching from an autocratic style must be progressive, since it may not be suitable for less experienced or less confident performers.

Having considered the various styles and approaches to coaching you are encouraged to reflect on the type of coach you think suits your character and the needs of your gymnasts. As you gain in experience and the relationship with your gymnasts develops you are encouraged to ask the gymnast what style of coaching they would prefer. You must be aware, however, that you should reflect on this situation continually as your gymnasts

develop, their needs change and how your approach to coaching needs to be amended to reflect these changes.

Key Points on Your Approach to Coaching

- Review and reflect on the coaching styles described above
- Choose a style that suits your character and motivation to coach
- Reflect upon the changing needs of your gymnasts as they gain experience
- Modify your style or approach to coaching according to the changing needs of your gymnasts – what is their preferred style of coaching?
- Reflect frequently on how effective your coaching style is, can it be improved?
- Remember your aim should be to help your gymnasts become self-sufficient.

Dealing with Coaching Challenges

In this section we will visit a number of challenging situations that you may need to resolve or deal with in your coaching career.

Coaching One on One

It is very rare in gymnastics that you will be in a situation where you will have a one-to-one gymnast-to-coach situation. This perhaps acceptable if the gymnast is an adult but it is recommended that you actually avoid even this situation since it leaves you with a dilemma on how you deal with a situation where one of those present has an accident or is taken ill. You cannot attend to the injured person and send for help on your own.

The situation is more complex if the gymnast is a child under the age of eighteen. In addition to the situation described above both people put themselves at risk of being accused of malpractice or even abuse. It is recommended strongly as a coach you never put yourself in this situation and you should always ensure there are always three people present at all times. It is advisable that at least two of those present are adults so that in the case of an accident, one can attend to the injured person while the other seeks help.

Coaching a Group

Whenever you have a number of individuals who constitute a group you will be faced with a range of abilities, different characters and individual needs. The challenge is to establish cohesion within the group in order to minimize conflicts or disharmony. As the coach to the group you will be required to show good leadership qualities that include:

- Setting individual and group goals
- Establishing standards of behaviour applicable to all without exception
- Demonstrating a positive attitude to training
- Providing encouragement and positive feedback
- Treating all individuals equally and with respect
- Demonstrating diplomacy
- Providing social support equally to each member of the group.

You may increase the possibility of creating group cohesion if you adopt the following tactics:

- When giving feedback, provide positive praise in front of the whole group (in public) but give criticism or reprimand in private
- Enable all group members to participate equally in group discussions
- Create an environment in which opinions can be expressed without fear of reprisal

- Promote group identity by using 'we' or 'us' rather than 'I' or 'me'
- Ensure that bullying does not occur
- Provide opportunities for group social events.

Resolving Conflicts

Situations may arise that result in conflict between group members, coaches, parents and officials. If you are called on to intervene to resolve the situation your strategies might include:

- Try to calm the immediate situation and address the issue away from the public view
- Clarify what the grievance is and seek the views of all individuals concerned
- Take time to consider your range of responses or actions
- Ensure your response is reasonable and proportionate
- Check your actions are understood clearly and not open to misinterpretation.

Reacting to Poor Performances

When your gymnasts experience poor performances in training or competition there will undoubtedly be feelings of disappointment. This calls for the coach to be supportive, tactful and intervene sensitively. Do not seek to apportion blame or put someone down.

Firstly offer support, give praise for effort and give yourself time to reflect on the situation. Your tactics might include asking questions to:

- Gain a sense of the level of perception of poor performance
- Identify the possible cause or causes.

Follow up the investigation with positive reinforcement of what went well and refocus the gymnast's attention on what needs to be addressed in training. Offer praise and encouragement to motivate the gymnast again.

Loss of Motivation of the Gymnast

Motivation is the process that inspires or gives incentive for someone to want to achieve something. Attaining a goal or learning a new skill may be the challenge set for the gymnast but the desire or determination to achieve the aim is what motivates him or her to strive towards successfully reaching the aim. Motivation is usually classified into two categories: extrinsic motivation and intrinsic motivation.

Extrinsic or external motivation is the form of motivation that comes from outside the gymnast and includes such sources as an inspirational coach, encouraging parent or fellow gymnast, and may involve some type of external reward such as winning a medal or earning a championship title. The promise of a present or prize, perhaps from a parent, as a reward for some level of success is clearly an incentive to do well but if the goal set is not that set by the coach and gymnast it may lead to disappointment all round.

Intrinsic or internal motivation comes from within the gymnast rather than from an external form. This personal desire to achieve a goal or target is perhaps the best form of motivation since the gymnast is motivated positively to work hard to achieve his or her optimum level of performance.

A good coach will endeavour to create internal motivation or self-motivation by continually offering encouragement and positive feedback to the gymnast. Discussing with the gymnast in a two-way democratic fashion what he or she wants to achieve and how they can realistically achieve those aims will help to inspire and motivate. Through this process, targets can be set that the gymnast believes are achievable and of real value to work towards. He or she will feel they have ownership of the goal and this will increase the personal desire and commitment to achieve the aim.

As a coach you will frequently be faced with the challenge that your gymnast becomes disenfranchised or loses motivation. There are many causes of loss of motivation that may include:

- Feelings of frustration due to lack of progress
- Boredom from a non-inspirational training programme
- Feelings of not being valued or respected by peers or the coach
- Frequently failing to achieve goals in competition.

Motivation can be enhanced by discussing and agreeing realistic goals with your gymnast. This will motivate the gymnast since he or she has been involved in setting the targets and will be inspired to produce the work ethic to achieve their aims. This important facet of coaching will be discussed more fully later.

Avoiding or Minimizing Loss of Motivation

If you can see or suspect that a gymnast has become demotivated, the first point is to be able to recognize the symptoms such as losing desire, losing work ethic, threatening to quit, making feeble excuses for failure, devaluing status or potential, or demonstrating emotional changes such as unhappiness.

Then you should raise the situation carefully and tactfully and listen intently to what the gymnast is expressing and experiencing. Let him or her know this not unusual, that most people encounter these problems at some point in their career but that the situation is not insurmountable. Dis-cuss why the situation might have arisen and how you might address the situation together.

Fear and Anxiety

Anxiety is usually caused by the gymnast being scared or in fear of something. It is manifested in tension, both psychologically and physically, and at the extreme in the refusal to perform a skill. There are numerous possible causes of anxiety in gymnastics and these may include a fear of:

- A particularly dangerous manoeuvre or combination of skills
- Falling, risk of injury or re-injuring a previously damaged body part
- Competition or failure in competition.

If we fail to prepare the gymnast suitably both physically and psychologically or fail to use the appropriate progression of sub-skills they may not be able to learn a skill safely and with correct technique. If we fail to allow the gymnasts to rehearse and consolidate a skill and try to progress them too quickly we leave

Table 2   Strategies for avoiding loss of motivation.

Symptom	Possible strategy

Frustration and lack of progress:
 	
• Goal or target may be unrealistically high
  Level of physical preparation may not be appropriate
  Sub skills may not be appropriate
	• Review the targets and set realistic goals
	• Improve the level of prerequisite specific physical preparation
	• Check the sequence of sub-skills is correct and rehearse and consolidate progressive sub-skills before moving on

Boredom with training due to: • Lack of motivation • Uninspiring goals • Repetition in the training programme	• Provide encouraging feedback • Review and set challenging targets/goals • Vary the content and sequence of the apparatus frequently
Feelings of not being valued: • Not being appreciated, valued or respected	• Show your appreciation frequently and praise the efforts of each gymnast • Encourage group co-operation and respect via group discussions and evaluation of effort from each gymnast
Failing to achieve competition goals: • Not gaining the expected level of performance in competition • Making mistakes frequently	• Review and reset the goals; are they realistic and in the control of the gymnast? • Discuss how he or she felt during the event and consider training coping strategies to overcome nervousness • Compare the success rate with that achieved in,training and perhaps reduce the content of the competition routine temporarily

them open to developing a fear of the movement and we put them at risk of injury.

It is extremely important that we always adhere to the good coaching practice guidelines to minimize the risk of the onset of fear.

The Recommended Sequence of Coaching a New Skill

1. Attainment of the appropriate, related, prerequisite skills
2. Development of a suitable level of specific physical preparation strength and flexibility
3. Ensure that the gymnast is prepared mentally and confident before progressing
4. Use a recognized sequence of progressive sub-skills
5. Allow sufficient training time to ensure consolidation at each stage of progression
6. Encourage rehearsal of previously learned sub-skills to reinforce safe and correct technique.

Loss in Confidence

Your gymnast will at some stage enter a period of loss in confidence or increased self-doubt usually brought about as a result of fear, a bad experience, confusion over a technique or lack of self-belief, which quite commonly manifests itself through increasing anxiety one week before a competition is due to take place.

This is where you are encouraged to introduce psychological coping strategies into your coaching regime in order to reinstate the self-belief into the gymnast. These coping skills might include:

Mental Rehearsal
This technique requires the gymnast to visualize him or herself performing the skill with confidence and good technique, and repeating this exercise until self-doubt is erased. This can be achieved by the gymnast feeling him or herself perform, or visualizing the performance mentally. This is like viewing a video or electronic recording of the performance. and may be applied to a single element or a full routine.

Positive Reinforcement
The gymnast rehearses the previously learned and mastered sub-skills that make up the particular whole skill to reinforce his or her ability and re-establish confidence to perform the skill or combination of skills.

Relaxation Techniques
The gymnast is encouraged to take him or herself mentally away from the stressful situation and visit a 'happy place' or one that is more peaceful and relaxing.

Positive Self-Talk
In this strategy the gymnast is encouraged to mentally or orally repeat a positive mantra such as 'I am relaxed', or 'I can do this', or 'I am confident' to improve their confidence.

Overzealous Parents

For a child to participate in gymnastics it may require many hours of training and time spent travelling to and from the gymnasium. This will entail great commitment and some degree of sacrifice from the parents and other family members. It may therefore be understandable that the parents feel there should be some return in the shape of progress for their commitment. Most parents are realistic and will trust in you to provide the best opportunity for the children to obtain their optimum level of participation. However, a minority of parents will show their frustrations openly if they become unsatisfied with the progress being shown by their child.

You will, I am sure, at some stage be faced with an overly ambitious, overzealous and unrealistic parent who believes his or her gifted child is underachieving and will apportion the blame to the coach. Often the parent will have overestimated the ability and desire of the child or have little understanding of the long term process involved in developing a young gymnast.

You can minimize the possibility of this scenario occurring if you talk openly and frankly to the parents of all your gymnasts, explaining:

- Your coaching philosophy and long term goals for the gymnasts and the club in general
- The developmental process and how progress will be influenced by the maturation rate and ability of the individual
- The predicted amount of training it will require to achieve a certain level of performance
- That you are approachable to discuss any concerns of the gymnast or his or her parents.

Remember to take time to discuss in private with the parents and with the individual, what are their ambitions and what you believe is the potential for that child. Do not criticize any child or their parents in public as this will only serve to exacerbate any issue or concern they may have. Be aware constantly of any rising concerns and deal with them at the earliest opportunity.

It is good practice for a club to appoint a gymnast or parent representative who can often dispel any concerns at an early stage or present any grievances to the senior coach or club manager. You may also find that if you hold regular club meetings for parents and coaching staff many of the misunderstandings can be clarified or avoided by those present being more informed about the circumstances. Experience will show that it is advisable to ask parents in advance of the meeting for any matters they wish to be included on the agenda. This will give you time to gather information and allow you to prepare for each item raised. Choose a diplomatic rather than an aggressive or authoritarian approach when discussing the issues. It is advisable to ask for those present to identify potential issues and possible solutions to the problems.

It is recognized that the coach's time is valuable and time spent at meetings is taking you away from training but time spent discussing issues openly with the gymnasts and their parents will reduce conflicts and ultimately enable the coach to spend more time in the gym without avoidable disruptions.

What to Coach

Introduction

We have looked previously at the 'how to coach' aspects of coaching, now we will describe the 'what to coach' concept. In gymnastics the 'what to coach' list includes many facets such as physical preparation (flexibility, strength and endurance), the essential foundation and core skills from which the many skills on each apparatus are then developed. A gymnastics coach must also learn how to teach a reasonable level of trampoline skills since this apparatus is used frequently as a rebound training aid through which aerial movements can be taught. Gymnastic coaches, particularly those in women's artistic gymnastics, will also need to be proficient in teaching dance and choreograph to enable them to prepare their gymnasts for routines on floor exercise and beam.

Physical Preparation Components

It is very important to remember that the well-being and safety of the gymnast is a priority and this principle can be upheld if we can ensure he or she is adequately mentally and physically prepared before starting to learn a new skill.

It is essential therefore to build into the coaching programme sufficient time to develop the level of physical fitness and strength progressively to ensure the gymnast's readiness to learn skills.

This will entail developing general fitness and endurance to sustain the length of the training sessions and must also include flexibility training to improve range of movement in the joint complexes. We must also ensure we develop a high level of general strength and specific strength (strength that is specific to the individual gymnastic skills the gymnast will learn). The different facets of flexibility and strength and the exercises and methods used to improve them will be dealt with separately later.

Foundation Skills

Foundation skills are the fundamental gymnastic movements that must be learned correctly to enable the more advanced skills to be developed effectively. These are best learned at a young age and include such skills as rolling forward and backward, jumping, landing, co-ordination, skipping, twisting, turning, and balancing on parts of the body. We will demonstrate how to coach these essential skills later.

Apparatus-Specific Gymnastic Skills

There are gymnastic skills that are specific to the individual apparatus and there are a few, such as the handstand, that are common to a number of apparatus. A selection of the more common and essential gymnastic elements will be illustrated later together with a description of the techniques used to perform them. The methodology of how to teach the skills will also be described.

CHAPTER 6

SPORTS PSYCHOLOGY

Factors Influencing How Gymnasts Learn

We have looked previously at the principles of how people learn but in order for us to provide the most effective coaching situation we need to consider other factors that will affect how the individual gymnast learns. You will be aware that we all have our own personality traits and will possess different levels of self-confidence. These may affect our motivation to learn, as will our personality and emotional state. A coach will therefore be more prepared if he or she has an understanding of these factors.

Personality Factors

The manner in which we behave and express ourselves may be classified in the following personality types:

The Introvert

This type of character is usually shy and quiet.

The Extrovert

The usual characteristics portrayed by an extrovert include being confident and outgoing.

The Introverted Extrovert

This character is normally quiet and withdrawn but when the environment is appropriate they become outgoing and confident. Gymnasts tend to belong to this category as in the training or competition environment they seem to have a change in personality from a normally quiet disposition to one of a confident and outgoing person.

Emotional Factors

Two emotional factors that may greatly undermine the ability of a gymnast to learn or perform gymnastic movements must also be considered.

Neurotic

This person is usually nervous and worries a great deal about what may happen.

Hypochondriac

This person will be oversensitive to pain and may overreact to injury. They may also show signs of depression.

These personality and emotional traits can also be exacerbated or influenced by other life factors, such as the onset of puberty or menstruation, family issues, problems with friends or pressures from schoolwork. During the period of puberty one should expect erratic changes in emotions from the adolescent gymnast.

Being aware of the personality characteristics should help a coach to be more understanding and supportive of the young gymnast and the coach should adapt his or her coaching style to suit the changing situation. An understanding coach will be approachable and able to discuss the situation in confidence, and will make adjustments to accommodate the emotional state of the gymnast. A coach who is in tune with the characteristics of the individual gymnast will also be able to adapt the frequency and style of presenting feedback accordingly. Some gymnasts will require frequent feedback of a positive nature to boost their confidence while others may respond well to less frequent feedback. Remember the praise sandwich when providing feedback: 'praise – corrective feedback – encouragement.'

Factors Affecting the Performance of the Gymnast

The performance of a gymnast may be affected greatly by such psychological influences as stress, fear, anxiety, fear of failure, fear of competition and self-confidence. Let us now consider how these facets may affect the performance and how we can prepare to reduce the adverse effects and indeed adopt strategies that can enhance the performance.

Anxiety

Anxiety is a state produced when we feel threatened by a situation that we interpret may affect our physical or social well-being adversely. We each have a different anxiety threshold level and are therefore more or less anxious according to how we perceive the threat. However, as the level of perceived threat increases, the level of anxiety increases and the performance may be affected badly.

It is import for a coach to be able to recognize the symptoms of stress and anxiety that may be evident as a high level of excitement, increased pulse rate, dilated pupils, a need to visit the toilet, sweating, tension in the muscles, dizziness and, in extreme cases, vomiting.

The likely causes of anxiety may include fear of injury, fear of competition, fear of losing, inappropriate thoughts, peer pressure, an overzealous coach or parent and unrealistic goals.

Stress

Stress occurs when someone is challenged by a task such as learning a new skill or performing a routine in competition. The individual will react according to how they see the threat or challenge. A high level of perceived threat may cause anxiety, resulting in nervous tension in the muscles or lack of confidence that may detract from the performance.

An appropriate level of stress may help to focus the mind and can increase the level of performance, but too great a level of stress can have an adverse effect.

Self-confidence

This is the belief that you can achieve something and can control the level of stress that the challenge may invoke in order to achieve the task.

Self-esteem

Self-esteem is how an individual sees him or herself as being respected by others or how he or she sees performance as being a success or a failure. This can affect greatly the level of self-confidence which, in turn, can affect the performance in a good or bad way.

Both self-esteem and self-confidence can be increased through encouragement and praise from the coach and other gymnasts. Being able to control anxiety and stress in order to achieve a task successfully will also lead to increased self-confidence and if the performance is praised by other gymnasts self-esteem will be enhanced. The overriding factor is how the individual perceives the situation in terms of success or attainment and this, in turn, can be influenced greatly by the level of the challenge.

Strategies for Dealing With or Coping with Anxiety

To achieve a high level of performance we must ensure the gymnast is prepared suitably both physically and mentally. The symptoms of desired level of mental or psychological readiness to perform are slight excitement, alertness, vitality, good concentration and a high degree of self-confidence. There are a number of recognized strategies or coping skills that can be learned and used to reduce stress and anxiety and these are described below.

Positive Self-Talk

This technique is centred on getting rid of or preventing negative thoughts from entering the mind. This is done by establishing positive thoughts or positive self-statements that help to increase confidence. Statements such as 'I can do this', 'I have done this before many times' and 'stay calm and remember to relax' are typical examples of positive self-statements. You must avoid statements that include 'I must not', 'remember not to' or 'don't do' as these are negative thoughts that can easily take control. The positive self-statement can be in the form of a mantra that can be repeated mentally or spoken.

Mental Rehearsal

This technique or strategy can be used as an aid to learning or improving self-confidence. Firstly, the gymnast should be relaxed and then he or she should visualize a successful performance of the gymnastics skill or routine and repeat this a number of times. The form that the mental imagery takes can be one of the following:

External Imagery

This is where the gymnast visually sees him or herself performing the skills or routine as someone else would see them, rather like seeing themselves on DVD or video.

Internal Imagery

In this technique the gymnast views an image as they would see themselves performing the skill.

Proprioceptive Imagery

This is where the sequence of 'feelings' within the muscles used to perform the skill is rehearsed. This can often be seen when a gymnast performs the sequence and pattern of arm movements required to create a twisting action.

It is possible that aspects from the three mental imagery techniques can be used together to good effect. Mental imagery is a very useful medium through which learning a new skill can be accelerated and the techniques can also be used to reinstate confidence when a previously learned movement has been lost or underperformed.

Using Goal Setting to Reduce Stress

One of the most effective strategies for reducing the negative effects of anxiety is to set appropriate training or competition goals or targets for your gymnast to work towards. To obtain best results from goal setting the use of short term, medium and long term goals is recommended. The long term goal is the end target or product you wish to attain and the short term goals are set for the imminent future. The medium term goals are interim targets that can be used to indicate the progress is on target midway through the learning process. Each of the goals should be related to the end product and should be suitably progressive. It is recommended that the coach should discuss the goals and agree goals with the individual gymnast as this will develop feelings of ownership of the goals and provide more determination and encouragement to achieve them.

A very good guide to developing appropriate goals is the SMARTER principle:

Specific: The goal should be specific, clear and precise

Measurable: It should be easy to measure so you will know how and when the target has been achieved

Agreed: The goal should be accepted and agreed by the gymnast and the coach

Realistic: The goal should be realistic and achievable with appropriate effort and determination. To provide the correct degree of motivation the goal must not be too easy or unrealistically difficult

Time phased: A suitable date for completion or attainment of the goal should be agreed

Exciting: The goal should be exciting and challenging to help to motivate and inspire the gymnast

Recorded: If the goal is written down it becomes a form of agreement or contract and this will enable the progress to be evaluated.

It is also extremely important that any goals set are in the control of the gymnast for them to be attainable. Setting a goal of winning a competition is not entirely in the control of the gymnast since he or she cannot control the performance of the other competitors or the scores the judges present. Your gymnast may have a terrific competition but there may be equally good or better performances from other competitors that merit better scores. The outcome may be that the goal is not achieved and your gymnast will be disappointed even though he or she had performed very well. Had you set a goal that entailed performing without a major mistake he or she would have achieved the goal and could be satisfied with the performance and gain motivation for the future. Let us consider the following goal: 'To perform the new floor routine in the regional championships on 10 July 20** and perform the routines without a major deduction (0.5 or higher).'

This goal is definitely in the control of the gymnast since he or she is the one performing the routine, but let us apply the SMARTER principles:

Specificity: Yes. The goal is specific and unambiguous; 'to perform the routine without any major deductions of 0.5 points or more'

Measurable: Yes. Are there any major errors in the performance, yes or no?

Agreed: Yes. The goal has been accepted by the gymnast and agreed with the coach

Realistic: Presumably the gymnast has performed the routine many times successfully in training and therefore with the right commitment and effort the goal can be achieved

Time phased: Yes. The routine is to be performed at the competition on a given date

Exciting: Yes. This is a new routine and will provide a sufficient challenge to excite and motivate the gymnast

Recorded: Yes. We can presume that the goal will have been agreed and written down so we can analyze the degree of success.

Goals can also be set in different contexts depending on what you wish to achieve.

Types of Goals

Outcome goals: These goals focus on the outcome or result rather than the quality of performance. A typical outcome goal would be 'to stick the landing' without stepping.

Process goal: This type of goal focuses on what to do in order to achieve an outcome or performance. 'Produce a powerful thrust at take-off to achieve sufficient height in flight to successfully perform a somersault' is one example of a process goal.

Performance goal: This type of goal is focused on the quality of performance rather than the result or outcome. 'To perform a skill without a bend at the knees' is a typical performance goal.

Remember that the goals need to have a purpose and the short term and medium term goals should relate to the long term goal to maintain motivation and ensure time is not wasted on distractions.

You may find it useful to explain the gym—nast's agreed goals to his or her parents to avoid the situation of the overzealous parent setting different goals and thereby placing a different emphasis on the gymnast's aims. You may have agreed a goal with the gymnast 'to perform without any major falls' but the parent may have made a deal with the gymnast to 'take them to their favourite restaurant if they win the competition'. These goals are in conflict with each other and while you may be delighted with the performance the gymnast may not be if they did not win the competition. We will revisit the process when we look at planning the training later.

KEY POINTS ON GOAL SETTING

The goals should be:

- Discussed and agreed with the gymnasts
- Be set according to the SMARTER principles
- Be sufficiently challenging to motivate the gymnasts to want to achieve them
- Be in the control of the gymnast.

CHAPTER 7

PLANNING THE TRAINING

The Principles of Planning

There are many views on the benefits of planning. Some people believe it is a waste of time since there are many factors that can change, such as an injury occurring or the gymnast becoming ill and missing training, causing the training plan to fail.

However, the author believes meticulous planning ensures every detail is considered in trying to facilitate the best possible chance of the gymnast achieving the optimum level of performance and success. If things are not planned then how do we know if things have gone wrong? After all, we can always adjust the plan to accommodate unforeseen or unpredictable events.

One effective way to approach the complex

Courtney Tulloch executing circles on the pommels.

process of planning the training is to consider the following questions. This is rather like planning a journey.

- Where are we now? What skills can the gymnast do at the present time?
- Where do we want to be? What do we want the gymnast to be able to perform?
- How do we get there? What programme of progressive training will achieve this goal?

If we can answer these questions then we can plan the journey through the training programme.

The process of planning can be as simple or complex as the situation demands but for the best results it is recommended that the recognized principles of planning are adhered to, as described below.

The Principles of Planning Sequence
- Assessment of the gymnast's ability and needs
- Target or goal to be achieved
- Planning
- Implementation of the plan
- Monitoring the effect of the plan
- Evaluating the outcome of the plan
- Reviewing and adjusting the plan.

The content and purpose of each of these stages of the planning process is described below.

Assessment of the Gymnast's Needs
The first stage is to gather and record as much information as possible on the current physical ability and stage of development of the gymnast – the 'where are we now?'

This may include what skills can the gymnast already perform, what is his or her level of physical preparation (i.e. flexibility and strength), how experienced is he or she, and

what stage of maturation has been reached? It is also very useful to identify what type of skill the gymnast has a penchant for, i.e. twisting or rotation, as these will be learned more easily.

The term used to describe the gathered performance information is 'gymnast profile' and this can be based on a number of recognized standard tests that will be described later.

Target or Goal Setting
The next stage is to plan 'where we want to be'. Here we can predict what the gymnast is able to achieve based upon his or her liking for certain types of skill and the demands of the competition judging code. These long term goals should be discussed and agreed between the coach and gymnast so the latter feels he or she has some level of ownership of the goals and will feel greater motivation towards achieving them. The goals must be realistic and achievable through commitment and effort to create the desired level of inspiration and motivation. We are now at the stage where we can 'plan the journey'.

Planning the Training or Competition Training Programme
This stage in the planning process involves setting firstly long term, then medium term and then short term training goals, and may contain the list of progressive stages of learning and volume of skills to be performed. The planned programme may be sub-divided into daily, weekly, monthly, yearly and four-year periods. These will be elaborated upon later.

Implementation and Monitoring
The planned programme is explained to all those involved and then implemented. At each stage of training the outcomes are recorded (monitored) against the previously agreed targets. Any deviation or incident, such

as injury to the gymnast, should be recorded as this may affect the success of the programme.

Training Programme Evaluation

The recorded results may now be evaluated to determine the degree of success of the programme. This will enable difficulties or problems to be identified, but it may also show areas of success that can be built upon or made greater use of in the next stage of planning.

Review and Evaluation

We can identify strengths and weaknesses in the programme and may consider whether we are on target, behind or ahead of the predicted targets and adjust accordingly.

Planning the Training Programme

Perhaps the most appropriate method of approaching the design of the training programme is to start with where you want to be at some time in the future and then to create the plan on how to reach your goal successfully. It is quite normal for the long term plan to range over a four-year period as this sits nicely with the four-year Olympic Games cycle.

The Long Term Plan

This four-year long term plan is often referred to as the macrocycle and sets out what are the goals to be achieved over this period. In competitive gymnastics the long term goals are usually represented by the routines the gymnast is expecting to perform successfully at the end of the cycle. This may be at the Olympic Games, for instance, but any relevant event may become the targeted competition. This four-year cycle is then subdivided

into small sections normally covering four one-year cycles.

The Year Plan

The twelve-month plan is usually referred to as the mesocycle and the first stage of planning it is to set out the competition or event calendar. The major competition for that year becomes the focal point when the date is inserted into the calendar. Preparatory events or competitions are selected as part of the build of experience and these should occur between six and two weeks prior to the main event. This gives the gymnast a chance to perform his or her routines in competition prior to the main event and enables the coach to evaluate the performances in the competition environment and to make adjustments to the training as needed. This period of the programme is referred to as the competition phase and this is one of four phases into which the mesocycle is divided.

The Four Phases of the Training Plan

Preparation Phase

This phase includes general physical preparation, such as endurance training, the rehearsal of core gymnastic skills and the development of new skills to be included into the competitive routines. It is usually six to eight weeks in duration.

Pre-competition Phase

This phase of training covers specific physical preparation relative to the skills in the programme, the perfection of skills and combination of skills and the rehearsal of part or half routines. The perfection of landings from the dismount are practised regularly in this phase. This period usually last between four to six weeks.

Competition Phase

The practice of full competitive routines to develop consistent high quality performances is the main focus during this phase. This, of course, includes the series of planned competitions each with its own designated set of goals designed to improve the awareness and confidence of the gymnast. This phase of training is usually scheduled to last around four weeks for best results.

Transition Phase

This is the period where the gymnast recovers from the intense period of competition training and will include rest to enable his or her body to recover and regenerate. Towards the end of this period the gymnast may commence general physical preparation and new skills may also be introduced.

The year plan or mesocycle described above is normally used for a young developing gymnast but as he or she becomes more advanced the year plan may be split into two cycles, each of approximately six months' duration. In this case each half-year cycle is subdivided into the four phases of training and the duration of each is reduced accordingly. The cycle is then repeated in the second half-year cycle. The advantage of the two-cycle year is that the gymnast and coach are able to test the programme and the competition routines in the first cycle and then make adjustments to enable the performance of the routines to be refined and consolidated in the second.

Week Plan

Once the various phases of training have been planned the programme can be further subdivided into week plans. These usually define the training days and rest days and

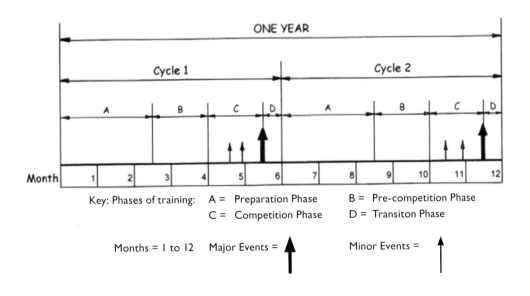

A typical two-cycle year plan.

outline the apparatus and total number of skills or routines to be performed over the seven-day period. It should be noted that the volume of skills to be performed on each day should be varied to provide high, medium and low load sessions to ensure the gymnast can recover between sessions. If this undulated balance is not built into the training programme the gymnast may become fatigued and the risk of injury or poor performance is increased.

Once the daily training demand has been established this can then be presented in the form of the daily training programme.

Daily Plan

This displays the order of apparatus or training station (physical preparation or ballet)

Table 3   A typical session plan.

Session Plan	Age of Gymnasts 9 to 10 years	Station Floor Exercise	Supported Handstand
Activity	Time	What to coach	How to Coach
Warm-up	10 minutes	Whole body, arms, legs and shoulders	Ensure gymnast active and uses progressive exercises
Core strength	5 minutes	Mid body front dish	Correct shapes, no arch in lower back
		Back arch held Standing stretched, body straight	Hold for 10 to 20 seconds
Main skill	30 minutes	Load bearing on hands	Bunny hops Tucked hand balance with partner Slow kick towards supported handstand
		Body tension	Lift feet around elbow support Partner supports at lower legs
		Kick to supported handstand	Body should not be arched Lead with shoulders Press down through arms Hold 3 seconds Lower single leg to floor
Summary and warm down	5 minutes	Give key points	Give praise and outline next skill to be learned
Appraisal of session session plan		Coach self-appraisal	

to be trained that day and it also indicates the list of skills (or routines) and the number of repetitions to be performed at each station.

Training Diary

To ensure the gymnast retains his or her motivation the content of the plan, particularly the day and weekly plan, is included in a personalized gymnast's training diary. The gymnast is able to monitor and record the volume and success rate of his or her performance on a daily and weekly basis. The coach can then analyze this record of performance and evaluate the degree of progress and success of the training period over time. The gymnast should also be encouraged to record any feedback or useful coaching points provided by the coach.

Session Planning

We have explained the principles of how to plan the training and how gymnasts learn the skills have been considered. It is equally important that we plan the individual training sessions carefully.

Session plans can be produced in the form of a spreadsheet or table and should include information such as:

- Title: apparatus or training situation
- Age or ability of gymnast to whom the session is relevant
- A description of the activity
- Time allocation for each element of the session
- Apparatus set-up
- What to coach: series of progressive tasks
- How to coach: key teaching points
- Session evaluation
- Coach self-reflection.

Key Points on Planning
- Fail to plan and you plan to fail
- Plan long term through to short term
- Long, medium and short term goals should be related
- Planning includes implementation, monitoring, evaluation and reviewing.

It need not be time consuming – plan to suit your needs.

CHAPTER 8

DEVELOPING RANGE OF MOVEMENT

The ability to move the limbs through the full range of movement (ROM), or in other words being flexible in each of the joint complexes, is a distinct advantage for a gymnast. A good range of movement enables him or her to learn and perform certain skills with correct technique more easily and may also reduce the risk of injury.

It is generally recognized that developing the ROM through flexibility training is best achieved in young children, usually before the age of ten or eleven. This is because later in the growth cycle and maturation stages the ligaments and tendons of the growing body naturally become much more resilient and stronger. It should also be noted the components of the body that limit the range of movement in a joint are the muscles, tendons, ligaments and connective tissue surrounding the joint. Each of these can be carefully

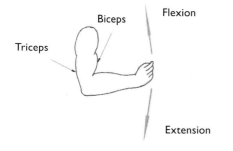

The flexion of the elbow joint.

stretched to some degree in the young but ultimately it is the configuration of the bones that make up the joint complex that limits the degree of movement in the joint.

Before we look at the methods used to improve ROM we need to understand a little of how the muscles react when we try to stretch them.

First we will need to understand a little about basic anatomy and how muscles function to cause the limbs of the body to move and how we can control the speed of the movement of the limbs.

Throughout the body muscles work in pairs to flex and extend the joints. When the brain sends an impulse to the muscle it stimulates the muscle to contract. The contracting muscle causing flexion is said to act as the **agonist**. Its opposing muscle in the pair must relax to allow the limb to move and this muscle is said to be the **antagonist**.

In the case of the elbow joint the main muscles that work as a pair are the **triceps** and **biceps**. To create flexion at the elbow, the biceps is the agonist that must shorten to cause the forearm to move upward around the elbow joint. At the same time its opposite muscle in the pair, the triceps, becomes the antagonist that must relax to allow the forearm to pivot at the elbow joint.

In order to create an extension in the elbow joint the roles of the pair of muscles reverses and the triceps muscle becomes the agonist that must be contracted while the biceps becomes the antagonist and relaxes to permit the forearm to rotate about the elbow.

Another 'pair' of muscles includes the **quadriceps** and the **hamstrings**, which act to create flexion and extension of the lower leg about the knee joint.

The quadriceps act as the agonist to cause the lower leg to extend about the knee and the hamstrings become the antagonist muscles to allow the lower leg to flex. If we wish to stretch the hamstrings we must contract the quadriceps and the stronger the contraction the more the opposite muscle, the hamstring, will relax. This makes it much easier and less painful to stretch the hamstring muscles.

This factor is very important when we attempt to improve the range of movement through flexibility training.

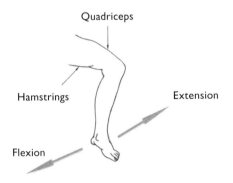

How the quadriceps and hamstrings control the knee joint.

Another important factor to consider when we stretch a muscle is the length of stretch and the rate or speed at which the muscle is being stretched. When a muscle is being stretched it is similar to an elastic band in that the further we extend the muscle

the greater the tension becomes. However, the body is so refined that as we extend the muscle it will tend to protect itself by trying to reduce the tension by attempting internally to contract in the opposite direction. The scientific term for this is the 'myotatic reflex', but is more commonly referred to by coaches as the 'stretch reflex'.

The Stretch Reflex

The muscle sheath is attached to a bone at each end by means of the tendon and as the muscle is extended the sensory spindles inside the muscle fibres sense the length and rate at which the muscle fibres are being stretched. The nerves that are attached to the sensory spindles send a message to the brain causing it to attempt to protect the muscle fibres by creating a tension in the opposite direction to the rapid stretch. The degree of response of the stretch reflex is proportional to the rate of stretch being applied to the muscle.

When we try to improve the ROM in a muscle or group of muscles we must stretch it beyond its normal relaxed length, known as its habitual length. This tends to cause 'slippage' between the muscle fibres in order to allow the muscle to become a little longer in length. This slippage tends to weaken the muscles

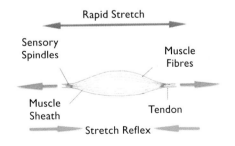

The stretch reflex action on the muscle.

55

temporarily, hence we should not plan or expect our gymnast to perform powerful or dynamic skills immediately following flexibility training. The muscle fibres will adapt to this situation by restoring the bond between the fibres over time. This factor has an important influence over when we should carry out flexibility training.

It is recommended that flexibility training is best included as a separate training session or after the main technical training, just before the cool down. This does not mean general muscle stretching should be removed from the pre-session warm-up. The warm-up stretching exercises should only be done within the full range of movement and are not intended to improve the flexibility beyond that point.

It is important to note that if we hold the stretching exercise for more than ten seconds in a prolonged hold we may begin to stretch the tendons as well as the muscles. If we repeat the prolonged hold of the stretching exercise a number of times this will improve the stretch placed on the tendons. This repetition of the stretching exercise is referred to as cyclic stretching.

We have learned in the previous section that muscles work in pairs and that to stretch one muscle we must contract its partner muscle to get the targeted muscle to relax. If we wish to stretch the hamstring muscles then we must contract the quadriceps muscles. Therefore, when we are attempting to improve flexibility we are really stretching the antagonist muscles as the targeted muscle.

We have also discovered if we stretch the targeted muscle rapidly it will incur a stretch reflex action that will inhibit the ability to stretch the targeted muscle. It is therefore imperative that when attempting to improve flexibility we must stretch the muscle slowly and progressively. Another import factor to consider when attempting to improve the ROM is that muscles tend to be more susceptible to being stretched if they are warm.

It is very important to remember that we must ensure the gymnast is warmed up fully before he or she begins the flexibility training. It is also recommended that we include the flexibility training session after the technical part of the session and just prior to the cool down section. It must be remembered that when we extend the full range of a muscle the overlap between the muscle fibres will be weakened temporarily so it would not be good practice to include flexibility training before the dynamic technical section in the training programme.

Methods Used to Improve Range of Movement

There are a number of different methods that can be used to develop ROM or flexibility in a gymnast. Each of the exercises will be based around some or all of the principles described above.

Ballistic Stretching

This method is often called dynamic stretching and involves swinging or moving a limb with momentum towards its full range of movement. Swinging the leg to the side, to the front or to the rear are typical of ballistic stretching exercises. This type of dynamic exercise tends to invoke a stretch reflex and they are not very useful when trying to improve ROM.

They are, however, a good warm-up exercise providing the full range of movement is not exceeded. This type of exercise can help to develop sufficient leg strength to enable the gymnast to lift the limb towards the full range of movement. This is called active range of movement and will be explained more fully later in this section.

Passive Stretching

As the name suggests, the gymnast attempts to remain passive throughout the exercise and should try to relax the targeted antagonist muscles in order to minimize the stretch reflex action. A gradual and appropriate external force is then applied to move the limb gradually and progressively to improve the range of movement.

Stretching the hamstrings and lower back muscles: The illustration shows the partner pressing down, with a suitable force, on the lower back to stretch the hamstrings and lower back muscles of the gymnast, who must attempt to relax the targeted muscles.

Active Stretching

In the active stretching method the gymnast contracts the agonist muscles actively to cause the targeted antagonist muscles to relax. In the illustration below the gymnast is targeting a stretch of the hamstring and lower back muscle groups and must therefore contract the quadriceps and abdominal muscles to create the desired effect. The effect of grasping the behind lower leg helps the gymnast to hold the position for a prolonged stretch.

Passive stretching with a partner.

Proprioceptor Neuromuscular Facilitation (PNF Stretching)

This rather long name is commonly referred to as PNF stretching and is a very effective method of improving flexibility. This method should be used only with more experienced gymnasts who can be trusted to act responsibly.

PNF Stretching of the Hamstrings

Gymnast A

Gymnast B

PNF stretching of the hamstrings.

In the illustration the PNF method is being used to improve the ROM in the targeted muscles, the hamstrings and muscles of the hips. The sequence used in the PNF method is:

An active stretch of the lower back and hamstrings.

- Gymnast A stands against a suitable resistance such as wall bars or a balance beam and lifts the leg as far as possible
- The coach or Gymnast B further raises the leg until he or she feels some resistance in the range of movement
- Gymnast B holds the position of Gymnast A's leg and Gymnast A presses downwards against the resistance from Gymnast B. Gymnast A will, in fact, be contracting the hamstring and gluteal muscles strongly in an attempt to press his or her leg down
- Gymnast A relaxes the muscular contraction slowly and Gymnast B immediately raises the leg upward a little until a resistance is felt
- Gymnast B holds the new position of the leg and the cycle is then repeated at least three times.

It is important to remember to stretch both legs and both sides of the body equally.

Active Range of Movement

It is equally important that we develop the gymnast's ability and strength to lift or move the limbs through the required ROM simultaneously. This ability is called the active ROM and is achieved by the gymnast actively lifting the limb to the full range and holding the end position for at least three seconds. The exercise is then repeated at least three times. The development of active ROM will be further explained in more detail in the section on strength training.

Examples of Flexibility Training Exercise

The illustrations below are examples of stretching or flexibility training exercises that can be used to develop the range of movement in each of the joint complexes. These are only a few examples and there are many other exercises to choose from. The exercises are typically used as 'slow, progressive and prolonged hold' passive or active stretching exercises but those involving partners could be adapted for PNF stretching.

Stretching the Hamstrings and Lower Back Muscles

1. Press the legs straight and reach as far backward with the fingers as possible.
2. Grip the underside of the bench and press the legs straight.
3. The partner places the hands on the lower back (not the upper back) and gently presses the torso towards the legs, which must be held straight.

1. Hamstring stretch.

2. Using a bench to stretch the hamstrings.

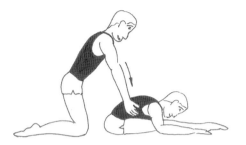

3. Partner stretch.

3. Bridge stretch.

Stretching the Shoulders

1. The arms should be stretched backward with the fingers touching. Use the legs to pull the body towards the heels to increase the stretch.

1. Shoulder stretch.

2. The partner overlaps the gymnast's arms and places the hands behind the shoulders and, with the help of the knees, pushes the gymnast's chest forward while pulling the arms backward.

3. The gymnast presses into the 'bridge' position that must be with straight legs and only slightly arched mid-body. The partner then places the hands under the shoulders and gently pulls the gymnast's chest towards them.

Stretching the Legs and Hips into Forward Splits

1. The front leg can be placed on a small block and the chest should be firstly leaned forward to stretch the muscles of the front leg. The shoulders are then moved slowly backward to stretch the muscles on the rear leg. The alignment of the hips should held in line for best results.

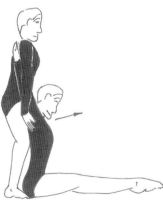

2. Partner shoulder stretch.

1. Forward splits stretching.

59

2. An excellent way of ensuring that the hips are in the correct alignment is to ask the gymnast to bend the rear leg at the knee. The heel of the rear leg should point upward if the hip alignment is correct. It is useful to get the gymnast to hold the rear leg in the vertical position while stretching the splits. Remember to stretch both legs equally.

2. Splits with rear leg bent.

3. The gymnast should lie down on the back with the arms spread wide to prevent the body from twisting. The partner then takes hold of the foot and heel of the leg and gently presses the leg towards the chest and holds the end position. This may be performed as a passive stretch or can be adapted to a PNF stretch with the partner offering the resistance.

3. Partner stretch for splits.

Stretching Exercises for Side or Box Splits

1. The coach or partner supports the gymnast under the arms and gradually reduces the support to allow the 'force of gravity' and gymnast's body weight to apply a downward force in order to push the feet further apart. This is a passive exercise so the gymnast should try to relax. The feet and legs should be in line with the hips in this exercise.

1. Box or side splits.

2. In this passive exercise the force of gravity and hence the gymnast's body weight will pull the hips downwards to stretch the inner legs and hips. The gymnast may also move the hips forward and backward gently to enhance the stretch.

2. Side splits on platforms.

3. The gymnast sits with the legs straddled wide open. The partner then places
the hands on the lower back and gently
presses the gymnast's chest towards the
floor between the legs. As the range of
movement improves the gymnast must
gradually open the legs wider until the
exercise can be performed with them in
the side splits position.

3. Partner-assisted side splits.

THE KEY POINTS TO REMEMBER FOR FLEXIBILITY TRAINING

- Warm up: Raise the body and muscle temperature by general warm up activity
- Use slow and progressive stretching exercises: Stretch the muscles slowly to avoid the stretch reflex action and progress the ROM over time
- Include flexibility training at the end of the technical section
- Try to ensure you develop full ROM in the early years of childhood
- Maintain ROM by frequent stretching sessions throughout the gymnast's career
- Use gentle progressive force to stretch the muscles. Stretching exercises will cause some discomfort to the gymnast but they should not enter the boundaries of pain
- Prolonged hold and cyclic exercises will help to stretch the tendons
- Flexibility is not generic. Some children are naturally more flexible but even though they may be flexible in one joint complex you should not assume this will apply to all their joints.

CHAPTER 9

DEVELOPING STRENGTH AND ENDURANCE

Previously, we introduced the principle that gymnasts need to be prepared both physically and mentally to enable them to learn and perform gymnastic skills safely. In the previous section we looked at flexibility training and how this benefits the ability to perform skills. In this section we shall describe the essential aspects of strength and endurance and how to develop these important factors in the gymnast's physical profile.

To understand fully how we can improve strength, it is important to be aware of how muscles operate to overcome a resistance to produce movement. The nerve cells are linked to muscle cells and each of these links is called a motor unit. Each motor unit will contract with maximum force when stimulated by the brain. When we wish to move a limb, say the flexion of the forearm about the elbow, the nerve senses the level of resistance and will recruit the required number of motor units in the muscle to overcome the resistance. The greater the resistance, the higher the number of motor units that are stimulated or recruited. Usually only 70 per cent of the motor units are recruited to produce a maximum contraction. The remaining 30 per cent are held in reserve to substitute the motor units as they become fatigued. Through training we can increase the proportion of motor unit recruitment to around 80 per cent to improve the maximum force the muscle can produce.

As a coach you will no doubt be aware that some athletes are able to produce very rapid movements (speed and power) while others are more suited to slow movements and repeat these over long periods (endurance). To produce rapid movements, the body needs fast twitch muscle fibres and to sustain prolonged periods of lighter effort the body needs slow twitch fibres.

The proportion of fast twitch and slow twitch muscles is hereditary and consequently we are all predisposed towards a particular sport depending upon the mix of fast and slow twitch fibres. Gymnasts tend to need a relatively high proportion of fast twitch muscles while long distance runners need a higher proportion of slow twitch fibres.

We can train to improve the strength and endurance of the muscles but we need to train the fast twitch and slow twitch muscles differently. Generally we will need to train the fast twitch muscles to produced high forces rapidly by using medium to high loads for fast but short periods. The slow twitch muscles are better for endurance and we therefore tend to train them with lighter loads over longer periods. From this explanation you may deduce that we need to train the different types of muscle in specific ways. We will revisit this fact later in this section.

The Principles of Strength Training

In order to improve the strength of a muscle or group of muscles we must increase the demand placed upon the muscles gradually over a period of time. By increasing the load or resistance progressively the muscle will adapt by increasing the cross sectional area of the muscle fibres to allow it to produce a greater force. This increases the girth of the muscle and is referred to as muscle hypertrophy.

We have discovered that if we wish to increase the strength of a muscle we must increase the demands on it gradually by a particular training method that depends on the load and duration. This principle is extremely important in strength training and is the essence of the principle that the muscles will 'specifically adapt to imposed demands'. This is commonly referred to as the SAID principle. Consequently, we must train for power, maximum strength and endurance through different methods.

We have mentioned that to develop each form of strength we need to increase steadily the demands on the muscles. In fact, what we will be doing is increasing gradually the loading on the muscles to cause them to partially fatigue. This principle of loading the muscle into the fatigue zone is called **The overload principle**. We must not misinterpret the overload principle as being excessively loading the muscles as this may lead to total fatigue and possibly injury.

Regular strength training will also improve the rate at which the muscle fibres can be recruited and the synchronization or efficiency of the muscles will also improve.

Types of Muscular Contractions

For the body to move the limbs effectively in different ways we need the muscles to work in various ways. As one muscle (the agonist) is contracting, its partner (the antagonist) must extend. If we wish to hold a static position we must fix the length of the muscle. The three main types of muscle action are:

Concentric Contraction

The particular muscle is contracted with the desired force and speed to shorten the muscle. Example: flexion of the forearm.

Eccentric Extension

The partner muscle must extend with controlled tension to allow the limb to move with the desired speed and control. Example: extension of the forearm.

Isometric Contraction

In order to fix or hold the position of a limb the muscle length must remain constant and this requires tension in the muscles to be maintained. Example: holding the position of a partially flexed forearm.

Each of the three forms of muscle action must be trained in different and in specific ways as described later.

Methods of Strength Training

A gymnast's physical profile will include range of movement, maximum strength, speed, power, muscular endurance and anaerobic and aerobic fitness. Each of the aspects of physical preparation must be trained in a specific way and in gymnastics it is recommended that we use the gymnast's body as the main resistance load. The resistance can be varied by inclining the body, altering the leverage or adding weight belts to the gymnast's body. The exercises we use should simulate closely the gymnastic skills we wish to teach the gymnast to produce maximum benefits. The methods used to train the various aspects of strength and endurance are described below.

Maximum Strength Training

This may be described as the maximum force that a muscle or group of muscles can produce to move a resistance load. This will usually require between 70 and 80 per cent of motor units to be recruited to produce this maximum force through contraction of the muscle.

The maximum strength can be improved by taking a near maximum load (usually between 80 and 100 per cent of maximum load) and performing three sets of the exercise, each set comprising between one to six repetitions. The load or demand should be increased progressively over time to increase the maximum strength in the particular targeted group of muscles gradually.

Speed and Power Training

To produce fast dynamic movements we need to develop power strength and improve the speed at which we can produce the required movement.

We can specifically train power strength by performing four to five sets of explosive exercises with a medium resistance of 50 to 80 per cent of maximum load. Each set comprises six to ten repetitions of the exercise that must be performed with accurate technique to gain maximum benefit.

Strength Endurance Training

Gymnastic training requires the gymnast to be able to perform a number of consecutive skills or routines over and over again without fatigue setting in. If the muscles tire quickly the performance deteriorates proportionally and the training may become dangerous.

The more repetitions of a skill or routine the gymnast can perform with good technique, the faster they will learn with less risk of injury

occurring. The gymnast will naturally gain in endurance through the performance of many repetitions of the skill but we can enhance the level of fitness by supplementing the training with specific strength endurance training.

There are two training methods that can be used to develop strength endurance.

Interval Training

An exercise that involves a light loading of between 25 to 50 per cent of maximum load is repeated between twenty and thirty times in one set. Up to five sets are performed with rest intervals of 30 to 60 seconds introduced between each set of exercises. The rest period allows the muscles to recover before being loaded again. As the level of fitness improves the number of repetitions in each set can be increased gradually to raise the demand and/or the duration of the rest interlude can be reduced gradually. The faster rate at which the gymnast recovers is generally a good indication that fitness levels are improving. Interval training helps to increase the endurance strength in the particular group of muscles used to perform the exercise that should be chosen to replicate a gymnastic action or movement.

Circuit Training

This method of endurance training involves the use of a variety of exercises each involving different groups of muscles in a series of exercise stations and is particularly useful for developing general muscular endurance.

The time spent on each station is set to suit the fitness and ability level of the gymnast and will vary between 15 and 30 seconds. The number of repetitions at each individual exercise station should be selected to suit the individual gymnast. Rest periods of between 20 and 30 seconds will follow each bout of exercise and between each station.

As the level of endurance fitness improves the number of repetitions, the time spent exercising at each station and/or the duration of the rest interval can be varied. This will maintain the challenge for each gymnast and will reduce the onset of boredom.

Aerobic Fitness

When we do low intensity exercises the chemical energy stored in the muscles and liver uses oxygen in the blood to release the chemical energy to the muscles. The term aerobic refers to the use of oxygen in this chemical process. This form of energy release can sustain light exercise over prolonged periods in activities such as endurance training. Children naturally gain a high proportion of their energy from the aerobic energy release system.

Anaerobic Fitness

When we exercise more intensively the aerobic system cannot supply the energy fast enough and we rely upon the chemical energy stored in the muscles to supply the energy rapidly. This process does not rely upon oxygen to release the energy and is referred to as being anaerobic. The size of the muscle affects the amount of chemical energy the muscle can store and this source of energy can be depleted quickly. Children are normally less anaerobically fit since their muscles are relatively smaller and can store less chemical energy. The by-product of intense exercise is lactic acid and this can diminish the ability of the muscle to use its stored energy. This will lead towards fatigue in the muscles.

However, strength training will increase the bulk of the muscle and in turn the ability to store chemical energy will increase and the onset of fatigue will be delayed.

It should also be noted that if we follow high intensity, lactic acid producing exercises with bouts of low intensity exercises, the lactic acid is diffused into the blood.

Consequently, it is recommended the training sessions should be followed by a cool down or warm down involving low intensity exercises.

Typical Strength Training Exercises

The exercises illustrated below are used regularly in gymnastics physical preparation programmes and many can be adapted to suit the particular type of strength training by varying the load demand of the exercise.

Strengthening the Mid-Body

Mid-body, or 'core strength' as it is often known, is fundamental to the success of a gymnast. The ability to change rapidly or hold the 'shape' of the body is essential in gymnastic skills. The first set of exercises are static or held exercises that should be held progressively for up to 20 seconds.

Static Mid-Body Shapes

Arch shape.

Dish shape.

Front hold on elbows.

Partner assisted front hold.

Once the static shapes shown in the first four diagrams can be performed with ease, the demand can be increased by extending the leverage between the points of support or applying an external force.

Partner assisted side hold.

Front hold on hands.

Strengthening the Hip Flexors

Abdominal curls.

Front lever.

The abdominal curl can be progressive by performing it:

- down a declining platform
- on a level surface
- up an inclined platform as shown.

Vee sits.

Strengthening the
Lower Back

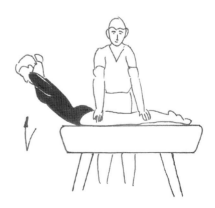

Leg lifts.

Upper back lifts.

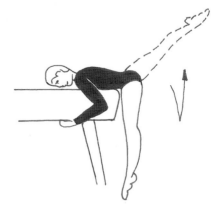

Lower back lifts.

Strengthening the Shoulders and Arms

Handstand push-ups.

Arm dips.

Strengthening the Legs

Arm pushes.

Hopping on one foot.

Rope climb.

Deep squats on one leg.

Sergeant jumps.

Plyometric Training

The majority of leg strengthening exercises involve some form of 'rebound' jumping, which is particularly required in tumbling skills or vaulting. The technical term for rebound jumping is plyometric training.

If the gymnast commences with a jump upward, then as her or she lands and bends the knees and ankles, the quadriceps on the front of the legs and tendons are stretched momentarily. This stored elastic energy is added to the rebound jump if it is performed immediately. The 'pre-stretched' quadriceps muscles and tendons can add up to 30 per cent more force than if a static jump were used.

The plyometric method is extremely efficient in developing strength and power but it should be used carefully as muscle soreness and possible injury can occur if the method is used to excess. Guidelines for the safe deployment of plyometric training are:

- Start with double leg springing with pre-pubescent or weaker children and progress to single leg hopping as they grow stronger
- Next introduce sergeant jumps and rebound jumps from a low platform, bench or box top of maximum height 40cm

Two leg rebound jumps.

Plyometric jumps.

- Increase the height of the platform gradually by increments of 10cm and rebound jump on to a second platform of equal height
- The height of the platforms may be increased eventually to 110cm and a good guide to adjusting the height of the platform is that the gymnast should be able to step down from the first platform and rebound jump on to the second platform immediately, without the heels touching the floor.

Training for Endurance

It is necessary for gymnasts to have a high level of muscular strength endurance and cardiovascular fitness (heart and lungs) for them to be able to sustain the demands of training and competition. Muscular strength endurance can be developed by interval training or circuit training, using the exercises shown above. The cardiovascular demands are at the greatest during the competition phase of training. In this phase the gymnast must rehearse many part and full routines and to meet the high physical demands he or she must develop good cardiovascular fitness prior to entering the competition phase.

In gymnastics we can achieve the required level of cardiovascular fitness or stamina through the following means:

Running or Jogging up to 3km

This form of general fitness training is best introduced to the training regime at the start of the annual programme in the transition phase. This will ensure the gymnast develops a good basic fitness level to enable him or her to meet the demands of the training programme right from the start of the season.

Repeated Performance of Basic Routines

Once the intended competition routines have been finalized the gymnast can perform 'reduced content' routines back to back to build up their cardiovascular and endurance fitness. These routines will resemble closely the structure of those intended for competition but the more advanced skills are replaced with similar more basic movements. This allows the gymnast to enter into the overload and fatigue zone without the risk of having to perform the advanced skills when tired.

This form of training must be included in the training programme towards the end of the preparation phase to ensure the gymnast is fit enough to meet the demands of the pre-competition phase and competition phase of training.

Key points for Strength Training Programmes

It is important to remember that all gymnasts are different and will have different strengths, weaknesses and needs. When designing a strength programme you must consider the following key points:

- **Assess the physical profile** of each gymnast or group of similar level gymnasts to identify their needs

- **Consider the age and stage of maturation** of the gymnast when selecting strength training exercises
- **Select training loads** that place sufficient but not excessive demands to create the required level of overload
- **Choose exercises** that simulate closely the gymnastic skills you wish to teach
- **Select the training method** to produce the desired effect: strength, endurance strength and so on
- **Arrange a circuit of exercises**, choosing the exercises that use the largest muscles first so as not to fatigue the smaller muscles before they are targeted
- **Cool down or warm down** after training to start the recovery process and diffuse lactic acid.

Strength training must be maintained otherwise the gymnast's strength and fitness will begin to drop after only seven days of inactivity.

CHAPTER 10

GOOD COACHING PRACTICE

It is imperative that coaches make the well-being and safety of the gymnasts their priority and this can be achieved by adhering to the recommended guidelines for good coaching practice.

Protection from Allegations

These guidelines will protect the coach from possible allegations of poor practice or abuse of the gymnasts.

- **Be open:** ensure your coaching sessions can always be viewed by parents or other coaches
- **Never coach one on one:** Make sure there is a minimum of three people present in the gym while you are coaching. Other than yourself, one of these should be a responsible adult. This will ensure emergency situations can be dealt with appropriately and you will safeguard yourself against any misunderstanding or allegations
- **Take care when supporting gymnasts:** Always used recommended methods when physically supporting children and if you accidentally touch a child in an inappropriate way report it to your club welfare office and inform the child's parents
- **Never make inappropriate remarks:** Never make sexually suggestive remarks to or about a child

- **Personal issues:** Never do things of an intimate personal nature for a child, unless you have been specifically requested to by the child's parent.
- **Inappropriate language:** Never use or allow swearing or inappropriate language to go unchallenged
- **Presence in the gym:** Always be present and available during your coaching sessions and never leave the gym at the end without ensuring the parents are present to pick up their children.

Providing a Safe Environment

Ultimately it is the owner or facility provider who is responsible for providing a safe facility. This includes the actual building and equipment. However, it is the responsibility of every coach to ensure the facility and equipment are used according to good safe practice guidelines. It is also the coach's responsibility to report and record any unsafe practice or damaged equipment. It is therefore important that you check the following regularly:

- **The facility:** Always check emergency exits are kept clear and heating, lighting, toilet and changing facilities are safe and clean
- **The gymnastics apparatus and equipment:** The coach must check the condition and safety of the matting,

apparatus, anchor points and training aids frequently and report any damaged or unsafe items

- **Emergency services:** Check the location of the nearest telephone, first aid box and qualified first aider in the facility.

Guidelines for Responding to Injury

If one of your gymnasts suffers an injury or serious mishap it is important you are able to deal with the situation calmly and efficiently and the following guidelines will help you:

- **Stop the activity:** When completed usher the gymnasts away from the scene of the incident
- **Check that the injured person is conscious and breathing:** This can be done by talking to them. If they are not breathing or they are unconscious send for trained medical help and commence emergency resuscitation or respiration as required
- **Ask what happened:** Establish the facts and ask if there is any pain. If you suspect a spinal injury **do not move the injured person** as any movement may exacerbate the injury. If the injured person is lying on a safety mat or a trampoline take care as you move around the scene as any movement of the surface may transfer to the injured person. Make sure any medical people attending the incident are aware of the need not to disturb the matting or trampoline
- **Look for signs of injury:** These could be deformity or abnormal movements of limbs
- **Keep the injured person warm:** Then, if in doubt, seek qualified medical assistance. Only after serious injury has

been ruled out should the injured person be moved

- **Contact the parents:** You should always notify the injured person's parents as soon as possible
- **Complete an accident report:** Whenever an accident or injury occurs you are advised to complete an accident form describing succinctly what happened and where and when the incident occurred.

Dealing with Basic Injuries

In any sporting activities incidents will occur that may require the coach to apply some basic first aid treatment and all are encouraged to train and become qualified as a basic first aider. Some reminders of the types of mishaps that may occur and how they can be dealt with safely are described below, but remember to wear medical protective gloves whenever possible:

- **Injuries to the skin** such as abrasions, blisters or torn hands should be cleaned with water and covered with a clean dressing. If the wound is bleeding place light pressure on the dressing over the wound
- **Injuries to soft tissue:** Injuries to pulled muscles, tendon strains or joint sprains should be treated immediately as follows by the **RICE** procedure.
  Rice: rest the injured part
  Ice: place an ice pack around the injured area but remember to wrap the pack in a towel to prevent ice burns to the skin. This will reduce bleeding and aid recovery
  Compression: bandage the injury firmly to reduce swelling
  Elevation: lift the injured part to prevent a rush of blood to the injured area.

The ice should be applied for between ten and twenty minutes every hour to reduce the bleeding and improve the rate of recovery. After thirty-six hours applying ice and elevation, the injury should be treated with alternate applications of ice and comfortable heat. The ice is applied for around five minutes followed by a heat pad for half an hour. This practice causes the blood vessels to dilate and this increases the blood circulation to aid the dispersal of any congealed blood that will impede the rate of recovery.

- **Impact injuries:** Accidents involving collisions with the apparatus may be treated by the application of an ice pack to reduce the bleeding. Blows to the head that show any signs of concussion should receive qualified medical attention.

Guidelines for Returning to Training after Injury

If the injury requires expert attention it is advisable to seek approval from a medical professional about when the gymnast can return to training. Firstly, when returning to training after injury, it is important to establish a relatively pain-free range of movement of a previously injured joint. Secondly, the gradual build-up of strength of the muscle surrounding the joint and the stability of the joint is assured. The level of demand from the training schedule can then be increased progressively. This procedure will ensure the injury is less likely to reoccur.

Guidelines for Providing Physical Support

It is quite usual in physical education and some less dangerous sports to encourage the participants to learn by a 'guided discovery'

method of learning. This teaching method may be applied to some of the fundamental movement skills in gymnastics but is not recommended for use with more complex ones. For the more difficult skills it is more common practice to provide physical support for the gymnast to ensure they learn them safely and with correct technique. The support from the coach should enable the gymnast to 'feel' the basic movement and technique required to perform the skill without greatly inhibiting the freedom of movement. Coaches in gymnastics are trained to use recommended techniques for supporting the gymnasts and the guidelines for the design and selection of the support technique are described below:

- Consider the point at which the gymnast may be at greatest risk or the point where support will best aid the gymnast to perform the skill safely with correct technique
- Determine whether the skill will involve the gymnast travelling horizontally and whether or not the coach will be required to travel with the gymnast to provide the required support
- Check that the base or supporting platform upon which you are to stand is stable so that you will not lose your balance and put yourself and the gymnast at risk
- Consider the need for a second supporter to assist you when the gymnast is too heavy for you to support safely by yourself
- Choose a suitable support technique from the recommended methods and ensure it will provide the necessary support without hindering the performance of the skill.

The recommended techniques for supporting gymnasts will be described in the section on teaching the various skills.

Guidelines for the Safe Coaching of Gymnastic Skills

It is recommended that when preparing to teach gymnastic skills you adopt the following stages in their planning and structured coaching:

- Firstly, ensure the gymnast is prepared both physically and mentally prior to introducing the new skill into the training programme. This should include flexibility and strength training specific to the skill
- Secondly, make sure the gymnast rehearses the core skills that form the foundations for the new skill. These core skills must be performed consistently with correct technique before introducing the next stage of progression
- Thirdly, select appropriate progressive **part skills** or **drills** that when perfected can be linked progressively or combined together to build up the whole skill
- Fourthly, allow time for the gymnast to develop consistency at each stage of progression before introducing the next progression. This factor is often overlooked but it is key in establishing a good base for further safe developments
- Fifthly, once the whole skill is performed consistently with support, the degree of physical support from the coach can be reduced gradually:
  - Full support provided throughout the skill
  - Light support at the key points in the skill, usually at the start or end point
  - 'Shadowing', not actually supporting the gymnast but following the movement of the skill and being alert and ready to provide support if required

- 'Spotting', being alert and ready to support at the end point or landing

Once the individual skills can be performed consistently without direct support they can be joined to form combinations of skills.

It is important to remember to expect a slight reduction in the quality of performance when skills are first joined together since the gymnast may be apprehensive about the progression. The coach should be alert to this situation and be ready to support if required.

The use of 'part skills' as progressions towards learning the full skill is highly recommended. This good coaching practice allows the part skills to be revisited or rehearsed if the gymnast's confidence or ability falters at any stage.

Guidelines for Setting Training Goals

It is important to note that individual gymnasts will have a preference or aptitude for certain types of skill and a good coach will discuss the selection of intended skills with him or her. This will encourage ownership of the training programme and this may increase the determination and motivation towards learning the new skill.

We have previously considered the SMARTER principles of goal setting and the influence this can have on the level of self or intrinsic motivation. A useful strategy for the use of goal setting in training is set out below.

Goals based upon **volume** of skills or attempts:

- Target the number of attempts at a skill or part skill at each approach to the apparatus.

Goal: 'make six attempts at a round off back flip on floor in a 30-minute session.'
- Set the total volume of attempts at the skill over a day or week
Goal: 'perform eighteen forward somersaults in a one-week period.'

Goals based upon **quality** of performance:

- Target the number of successful attempts at performing a skill.
Goal: 'perform three successful performances out of eight attempts at a skill in one 30-minute session.'
- Set the total number of successful routines over a one-week period
Goal: 'perform ten successful competition routines on beam/rings in a one-week period.'

In order for the goals to be specific and measurable the term 'successful' will need to be defined so the gymnast and coach agree on what constitutes a successful performance. Perhaps 'performing the skill without a fall or deduction of 0.5 points' will be sufficient to measure the performance.

When using quality-based performance goals while a skill is being learned the level of motivation can be maintained by increasing the target gradually. This can be done as follows:

1. 'Perform three successful performances from eight attempts.'
2. 'Perform four successful performances from eight attempts.'
3. 'Perform five successful performances from ten attempts.'
4. 'Perform six successful performances from ten attempts.'

Note the incremental changes are achievable and realistic, and allow for consolidation in the performance.

KEY POINTS IN GUIDELINES FOR COACHING PRACTICE

The guidelines described above are designed to protect both the gymnast and coach against allegation of poor practice and will also ensure the coaching will be effective.
  Remember to:

- Provide a safe environment at all times
- Ensure the gymnast's safety is paramount
- Never coach one on one and always ensure your sessions are open to be viewed
- Check the condition of the apparatus and training aids regularly
- Prepare your gymnast physically and mentally before introducing a new skill
- Always use recommended part/whole skill progressions
- Allow time for consolidation before moving to the next stage
- Use only recommended and recognized physical supporting techniques
- Set appropriate training goals to maintain the challenge and stimulate motivation.

CHAPTER 11

UNDERSTANDING BIOMECHANICAL PRINCIPLES

Mechanical principles are the scientific rules that describe how things work. When these principles are used to explain and measure how the human body works the term used to describe this field of science is biomechanical. A working understanding of these general principles will enhance greatly a coach's ability to understand and explain the key coaching points used in the correct performance of the gymnastic skills. Firstly, we need to be clear about the meaning of the basic terminology.

Biomechanics Terminology

Mass (m): The amount of matter a body possesses, measured in kilograms (kg).

Gravity (g): The force that attracts a body towards the centre of the earth. The gravitational force will accelerate a body vertically downwards at a rate of 9.81 metres per second. Hence the saying 'what goes up must come down'.

Centre of mass (c of m): The point at which all a body's mass could be considered to be concentrated and is an imaginary point through which a body can be balanced. In a straight body shape the c of m is on a line near to the navel. However, the position of the c of m will change depending on the distribution of the mass and may even be outside the body, as illustrated in

the arched or piked shape. Even raising the arms will lift the position of the c of m.

Velocity (v): The measure of how fast an object is moving and is measured in miles per hour (mph) or metres per second (mps) if the object is travelling in a straight line.

Acceleration (a): The measure of how quickly an object's velocity changes or how quickly its speed changes. Measured in metres per second per second (m/s/s). The opposite to acceleration is deceleration, a measure of how quickly a body is slowing down.

Angular velocity (av): If the object is rotating the speed of rotation is called the angular velocity.

Angular acceleration (aa): The measure of how quickly an object's speed of rotation changes.

Momentum (m): When a body of mass 'm' is moving at some speed (velocity 'v') it will develop motion and the measure of motion is momentum. The mass of the body will remain constant but the velocity may vary. Consequently, we can calculate the momentum that a body possesses because of its velocity by multiplying its mass by the velo-city.

Momentum = mass × velocity

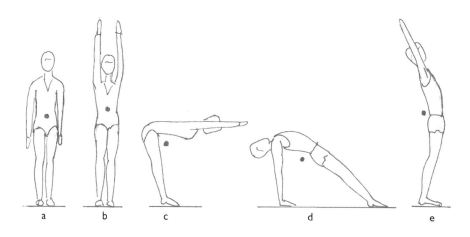

The position of the centre of mass.

Therefore:

- The faster a body is moving, the greater momentum it will possess
- The greater the momentum a body possesses the more difficult it is to slow down
- If two bodies of different mass are travelling at the same speed the heavier body will possess the greater momentum.

Force (f): To initiate movement a force must be applied to a body. The applied force tends to move the body in the direction in which the force is applied.

Now that we know the basic terminology we can begin to consider the biomechanical principles that are important when coaching gymnastic skills.

Newton's First Law of Motion

Newton's first law of motion is: 'A body will remain at rest or continue in a state of uniform motion in a straight line unless it is acted upon by an external force.'

In simple terms, if a body is already moving

and we apply an external force to that body this will alter its velocity. If the force is applied in the direction in which the body is moving it will increase the velocity. Conversely, if the force is applied in the opposite direction the force will tend to reduce the velocity of the body.

Newton's Second Law of Motion

If we apply sufficient force to a body it will cause a change in the velocity of movement, i.e. it will cause it to accelerate and the momentum of the body will alter. This then equates to Newton's second law of motion: 'The rate of change of momentum of a body is proportional to the force causing it and the change takes place in the direction of the applied force.'

Force = mass x acceleration

Newton's Third Law of Motion

This very important third law states that: 'To every action force, there is a reaction force that is equal in magnitude and opposite in direction to the applied force.'

In simple terms this can be interpreted as:

'For every force there is an equal and opposite reaction force.'

This can be explained simply in the following practical example shown in illustration. If the gymnast drives the arms momentarily in a forward direction, action force **A**, it will cause a reaction force **R** that is equal in magnitude to but opposite in direction to force **A**.

In the second diagram, if at the take-off from the floor the gymnast momentarily drives the arms upward, action force **A**, there will be an equal and opposite force reaction force **R** through the feet. This force **R** will in turn act against the floor and will result in another equal and opposite force from the floor against the gymnast's feet. This is called an **indirect reaction** force **IR** and will equal in magnitude to the initial force **A**.

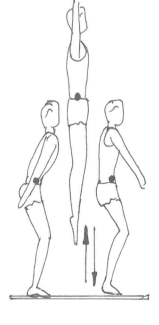

Action and reaction forces.

Indirect reaction force.

The Effect of the Force of Gravity

If the gymnast jumps upward vertically, the time spent rising from maximum velocity at take-off to zero velocity at the top of the flight will be exactly the same time as the time spent accelerating downwards to the floor. This is because when rising the force of gravity will be slowing down the velocity and when falling the force of gravity will be accelerating the velocity at exactly the same rate (9.81m/s/s) It is important to remember that, 'what goes up must come down' due to the effect of the force of gravity and this factor will influence the flight path of the c of m when a body is in flight. The time to rise will be the same as the time to fall.

The force of gravity.

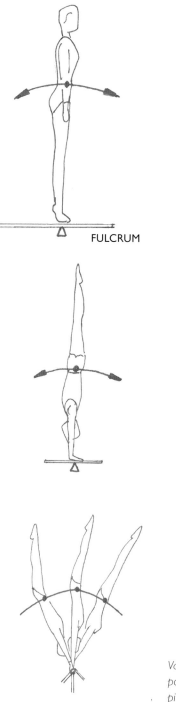

FULCRUM

Various points of pivot.

Rotational Motion

When a gymnast is in motion and in contact with an apparatus the body will 'pivot' about the point of contact with the apparatus, which may be called the fulcrum. The previous three illustrations show how the c of m pivots in this way.

Rotation and Flight

Let us now consider the situation when a gymnast is not in contact with the apparatus. When a gymnast is in flight any rotation the body possesses will cause it to rotate about its centre of mass. Once the gymnast loses contact with the floor or apparatus the force creating the rotation will cease to exist and the only force acting on the body will be the force of gravity. During flight the gymnast may be considered to be a projectile and the flight path of the c of m will follow a **parabolic** curve.

Parabolic Flight Path of the Centre of Mass

Some key points to note in relation to the illustration above:

1. At the point of take-off three combined factors will influence the flight path:
   - Reaction force **R1** will influence the upward velocity at take-off and consequently this will determine the duration of upward motion. The force of gravity will slow down the upward velocity to zero and then accelerate the downward velocity
   - The angle of take-off will dictate the initial direction of the flight path
   - Reaction force **R2** will add a turning effect through the feet to add to the degree of rotation momentum.
2. At the point of take-off the force **R2** will

The parabolic flight path of the c of m.

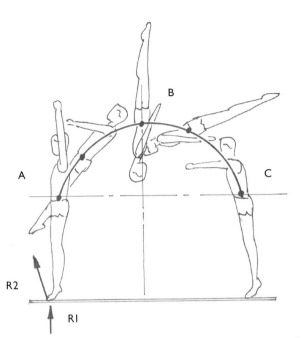

also influence the amount of somersault rotation by producing a 'turning moment' at the feet to increase the rotation about the c of m as the feet

leave the floor. It is important to maximize this turning effect by stretching the body and raising the arms during the take-off.

3. Once the feet lose contact with the floor the force of gravity will be the only force affecting the body and the flight path of the c of m will follow the parabolic curve. Consequently the time to rise from point A at take-off to point B, the top of the flight, will be exactly the same as the time to fall from point B to point C, the point of first contact with the floor.

4. The amount of rotational momentum of the body will be constant from the moment the feet leave the floor and will remain the same upon landing.

5. The speed of rotation (angular velocity) of the body can be altered during the flight by reducing the moment of inertia (resistance to rotation). This may be done by altering the position of the arms or varying the shape of the body (i.e. tucking or piking),but the angular momentum will remain the same.

Now let us consider what happens when a gymnast, who is rotating about the hands on a bar, releases his or her grasp to perform a dismount.

Flight Path of the C of M During a Dismount

The key points to note here are that:

- The gymnast will rotate around the hands on the bar and the c of mass will scribe a circle around the bar (if the body shape remains constant)
- At the point of release of the hands the c of m will initially travel tangentially to the circular motion around the bar. This means that the c of m will initially travel at 90 degrees to the point of the c of mass at release
- After release, the force of gravity will cause a parabolic flight path to occur and the c of m will follow that curve

81

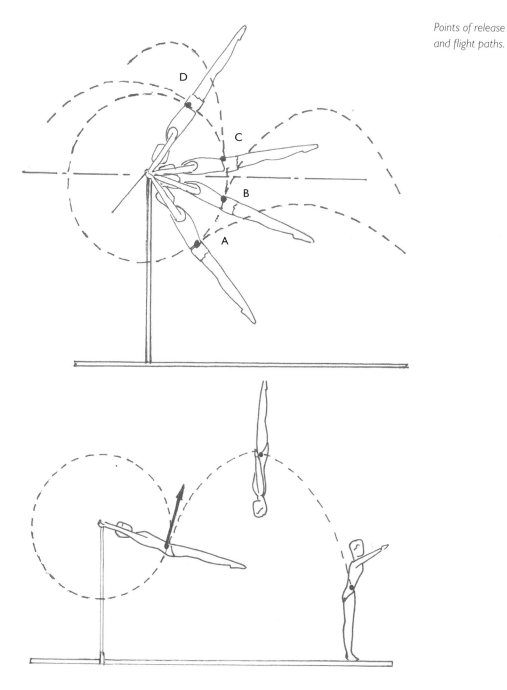

Points of release and flight paths.

Dismount flight path.

- The height and flight time of the c of m will be determined by the angle of release and the momentum possessed by the body at the time of release from the bar
- The amount of angular momentum will remain constant during the flight, but it should be noted that the time spent rising will be shorter in duration than the time spent falling owing to the position of the c of m on landing being lower than that when releasing the bar.

The Effect of Various Release Points

A. Early release will produce a lower and flatter trajectory
B. Release at just below horizontal with the bar produces the correct and safe flight path
C. Late release at above the horizontal will provide more height in flight but the body will tend to travel towards the bar
D. A release towards the vertical will tend to travel over the bar.

It should also be noted that the degree of angular momentum at the point of release will also affect the height and flight time of the parabolic curve. The greater the momentum, the longer it will take the force of gravity to slow down the momentum, hence the curve will tend to be higher and the flight time will be longer.

The Axes of the Body

It is possible to rotate about each of the three axes of the body as illustrated below.

Axis AA: The Lateral Axis. Such skills as forward and backward roll or somersaults rotate about this axis.

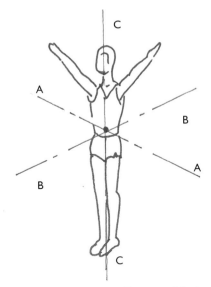

The axes of the body.

Axis BB: The Transverse Axis. The cartwheel and sideways somersaults rotate around this axis.

Axis CC: The Longitudinal or Vertical Axis. A spin or turn on floor or beam will rotate about the vertical axis.

The Mechanics of Twisting

A twist may be defined as being a rotation around the longitudinal axis of the body within a somersault and a twist may be created by different techniques: torque twist, hula twist and tilt twist.

The Torque Twist method
If we exert a turning force at a certain distance from the axis of rotation this will produce a turning moment about the axis. This in will produce an effect called a torque on the body.

If a gymnast pulls the arms wide and forces the arms in an anticlockwise direction (**A**) this

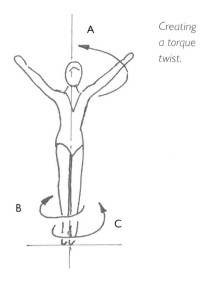

Creating a torque twist.

The Hula Twist Method

The hula method of creating a twist is also referred to as a 'two axis' twist as it involves displacing segments of the body in sequence about the longitudinal or vertical axis of the body. This can be explained and demonstrated with the gymnast hanging from a single still ring from both hands. If the gymnast introduces a slight arch into the body and then circles the hips in a clockwise direction (**CW**), sideways, to the rear, sideways and forward in a conical or hula action the gymnast will turn or twist in the opposite direction. (i.e. anticlockwise, **ACW**).

will produce an equal and opposite turning moment in a clockwise direction through the feet against the floor (**B**). This will result in a reaction that will be equal and opposite, causing an anticlockwise reaction turning moment (**C**) or torque through the feet to the body. Hence the result is a turn or twist in the anticlockwise direction. A torque twist is generated more easily when the feet or hands are in contact with an apparatus.

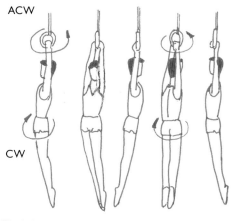

The hula twist.

Key Points for Generating Torque Twisting

- The wider the arms are placed the greater the torque achieved
- The torque should be initiated at the point furthest away from the point of contact with the apparatus: the hands lead when the feet are in contact with the apparatus; the feet lead when the hands are in contact with the apparatus
- Once contact with the apparatus ceases the arms should be drawn rapidly into the body to reduce the moment of inertia (resistance to rotation) in order to speed up the velocity of the twist rotation around the vertical axis.

The Hula or Two-Axis Twist

This method of twisting is based on the principle of 'conservation of momentum'. If the gymnast starts in a static position the angular momentum is zero. If the hips are then circled in a clockwise direction the body will twist in an anticlockwise direction in order that the angular momentum about the longitudinal axis remains zero.

It should be noted that if the hula action ceases then the twisting will stop immediately.

Key Points for Creating Hula Twist

- Circling the hips in one direction produces a twist in the opposite direction
- The twist will cease the moment the hula action of the hips stops.

Tilt Twisting Method of Producing Twist

This method of initiating a twist can work only if the gymnast has somersault rotation since it relies on the longitudinal axis of the body being 'tilted' away from the vertical somersault plane. The twist is produced by creating a difference in the resistance to rotation (moment of inertia) between each side of the body. This is created usually by dropping one arm, but it can also be created by raising one arm.

For the purposes of clarification we will describe the twist direction by referring to the backward movement of the shoulder such that:

- **In a clockwise twist the right shoulder moves backward, i.e. twist to the right**
- **In an anticlockwise twist the left shoulder moves backward. Twist to the left.**

Forward Somersault with Anticlockwise Twist

Imagine a gymnast somersaulting in a forward direction with the arms above the head, and then dropping the right arm to the side. The resistance to rotation on the right side of the body will now be less than that on the left side of the body. Consequently, the left side of the body will tend to rotate around the transverse axis more slowly than the right side. This causes the longitudinal axis of the body to tilt from the vertical plane and the right side will rotate faster in a forward direction. Hence the right shoulder moves forward and the left shoulder

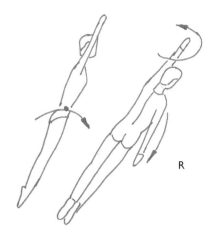

Forward tilt twist.

backward. This will cause a twist to the left.

Backward Somersault with Anticlockwise Twist

If a gymnast performs a backward rotating somersault with the arms initially above the head at take-off and then drops the left arm to the side, this will reduce the resistance to

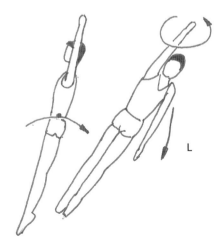

Backward tilt twist.

85

rotation on left side of the body and cause the left shoulder to move backward, creating a left twist or anticlockwise twist.

Key Points for Teaching a Somersault with Twist

We have considered the three common methods used to generate a twist around the longitudinal axis of the body and itshould be noted that the majority of twists usually incorporate one or more of them.

Torque Twisting

- Usually initiated while in contact with the apparatus (feet or hand contact)
- The torque twist is initiated by turning the part of the body furthest away from the point of contact with the apparatus.

Hula or Two-Axis Twisting

- Created by a 'hula' action of the hips
- The twist will occur in the opposite direct to the direction of rotation of the hips
- The hula twist will cease the moment the hip action is stopped. This is useful when preparing for the landing from a twist created by this method.

Tilt Twist

- Requires some somersault rotation for this method of twisting to be effective
- Once the twist has been initiated dropping the second hand and wrapping the arms into the body will increase the twist rotation
- The fact that the longitudinal axis tilts will cause the velocity of the somersault to increase
- On completion of the twist the arms can be lifted to reduce somersault rotation and opened wide simultaneously to reduce the speed of twist rotation in readiness for the landing.

Forward Somersault

- **Left Twist:** Drop the right arm or raise the left arm
- **Right Twist:** Drop the left arm or raise the right arm
- The entry into the forward somersault should be in a dished shape as this enables a hula twist to add to the efficiency of the twist.

Backward Somersault

- **Left Twist:** Drop the left arm or raise the right arm
- **Right Twist:** Drop the right arm or raise the left arm
- The entry into the backward somersault should be with an arched body shape as this will allow a hula action to assist with the twisting action.

Determining the Gymnast's Preferred Direction of Twist

Problems may be encountered when a gymnast begins to link skills that contain a twist if the direction of twist in the individual skills has been learned in a different direction.

Experience has shown that this potential problem can be avoided if we determine the natural or preferred direction of twist right from the start and then ensure the gymnast uses this twisting direction in all his or her skills.

The preferred direction of twist can usually be established through the use of three simple drills shown in the diagram.

Falling backward and making a half turn

Encourage the gymnast to fall backward about the feet and make a half turn without consciously thinking about the direction of turn. The landing should be on a safety mat with the fingers pointing forward.

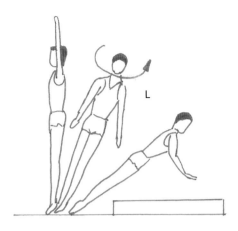

Falling backwards.

Falling Forward and Making a Half Turn

The gymnast should fall forward and make a half turn to land on a safety mat. The fingers

must point forward and the arms should absorb the momentum of the fall. Again, the half turn must be made without any predetermined direction and the direction of the turn noted.

Making a Jump Half Turn

The jump and half turn should be performed spontaneously and the direction of turn noted.

Hopefully the turns will all be made in the same direction, but if this is not the case the coach should select the more natural direction.

Once the preferred direction of twist has been determined always encourage the gymnast to use the same direction of twist when learning other skills.

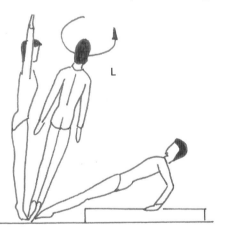

Falling forwards.

Jump half turn.

CHAPTER 12

COACHING THE GENERIC FOUNDATION SKILLS

The Generic Gymnastic Foundation Skills

There are certain basic gymnastic skills that underpin the learning of many of the more advanced ones and it is essential that these are learned early in a gymnast's career. These skills are described and illustrated in this section.

Learning to Fall Safely

It is extremely important we teach our gymnasts how to land and how to escape safely from an abortive attempt at a skill as this will avoid the fear of falling and reduce the risk of injury.

It is, of course, imperative we provide a suitable soft and absorbent surface around the apparatus to reduce the impact from landings or falls. This usually involves gymnastic mats, safety mattresses or pads being attached to the apparatus.

However, the key to falling safely is to attempt to reduce the impact of the landing or fall. This may be achieved by:

- Dissipating the landing force over as long a period of time as possible
- Spreading the impact over as much body surface as possible
- Avoid landing on straight legs or arms
- Absorbing the force of the landing or falling by controlled bending of the knees, ankles and hips when landing on the feet, or wrists and elbows when landing with hands down
- If necessary, protect the head and neck by cradling the arms over the head or, if appropriate, the gymnast may roll out of the fall with either a backward, forward or shoulder roll.

Falling Forward

Turn the hands inwards and control the bending of the elbows.

Landing falling forwards.

Falling Backward

The hands should point forward and control the bending at the elbows.

Landing falling backwards.

Turn and Fall

The gymnast may find it safer to make a half turn to fall forward.

Turn and fall.

Roll and Cradle the Neck

The gymnast should break the impact with controlled bending at the elbows, then cradle the hands quickly behind the neck.

Roll and cradle.

Recovery From an Over-balanced Handstand

When teaching a handstand balance it is important to teach the recommended safe methods of escaping from an over-balanced position to reduce the risk of injury. Two commonly used escape methods are shown below:

Rolling out of the Handstand

Upon overbalancing keep the arms straight and then gradually bend the arms, tuck the head under and tuck the body to forward roll out.

Handstand roll out.

Turning out of the Handstand

Step forward with one hand making a quarter turn and then lower the same leg as the stepping hand, towards the floor keeping the arms straight.

Coaching Safe Landings

The ability to land safely with control and with the correct technique is an essential

Handstand turn out.

requirement in gymnastics. This fundamental skill should be taught in the early stages and should be practised regularly throughout the gymnast's career. Not only will a good landing ensure fewer points are deducted in judging but the risk of injury will be reduced greatly.

Controlled Landing

The landing should first be introduced from a vertical jump. The contact with the floor must be with the balls of the feet and toes. The heels are lowered rapidly, the ankles, knees and hips are bent with control, and the arms are brought downward in front of the body to arrest the momentum.

Jump and land.

Improving Strength and Technique

The exercise shown should be carried out slowly with tension in the legs to improve strength and understanding of the technique. Repeat the exercise at least ten times and increase the resistance (loading) gradually by holding a weight in front of the body or fitting a weighted belt around the waist.

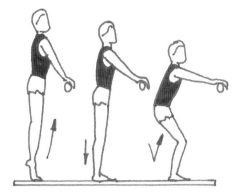

Leg squats and heel raises.

Jumping Forward from a Platform

Jumping upward and forward increases the downward force on the legs but also adds forward momentum to the flight. After the top of the flight the legs must move forward so the feet land in front of the centre of mass (c of m) of the body. This enables a force to be applied forward against the floor to produce an equal and opposite force from the floor to arrest the forward momentum of the body.

Jumping forwards from a platform.

Jumping Backward from a Platform

This offers another challenge since the momentum is in a backward direction. In the descent the feet must be moved backward so they land behind the c of m of the body. This enables a force to be applied in a backward direction against the floor to arrest the momentum.

Jump backwards from platform.

Changes in Shape and Direction

Changes in body shape such as a tuck, pike or twist can be added to give variety to the

Twisting and landing.

jump. This allows the gymnast to understand how to arrest the momentum when landing with slight sideways and twisting movements.

Landings from more advanced skills should be introduced as part of the progressive learning programme for each skill. This may include handsprings and forward or backward somersaults from a raised platform and dismounts from the apparatus. These should be practised throughout the learning and competitive stages of training to ensure the landings are safe and secure.

Handspring landing.

- If the c of m moves outside the area of the support base the body will tend to be off balance
- The larger the area of support base the easier it will to maintain the balance
- The closer the c of m is to the support base the more stable the body will be
- The centre of mass may be outside the body and remain on balance in certain shapes.

Tuck back landing.

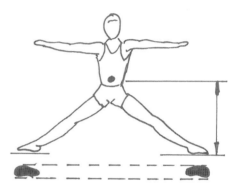

Straddle stand.

Coaching Balance

To be able to train balance effectively a coach needs to have some understanding of basic biomechanical principles, as described below:

Mass: The amount of matter a body possesses.
Centre of mass (c of m): The point at which the body's mass is concentrated and may be considered to be the point of balance of the body.
Support base: This is the perimeter or area within which the body is being supported.

Rules for Centre of Mass and Balance
- To remain on balance the centre of mass must stay inside the area of the support base

Standing erect.

In the straddle stand shape the wide spread of the feet produces a large support base area and the c of m is much closer to the base. This shape is therefore much more stable than in the standing position, where the support area is much less and the c of m is further from the base.

Consider the sequence of illustrations and notice the position of the c of m, which may be outside the body. Also note how the body shape must be repositioned to retain the balance with the c of m directly over the support base.

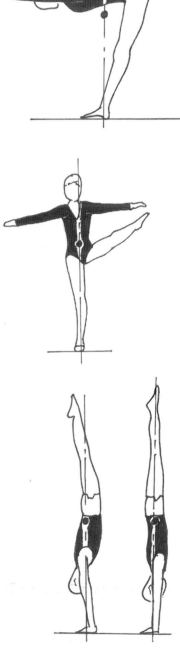

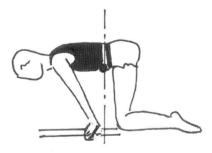

Position of centre of mass.

Coaching the Handstand

The handstand is perhaps the single most important gymnastics skill and, if learned correctly, will provide the gymnast with a strong foundation upon which many advanced skills can be based. Conversely, if it is not taught or learned correctly it will always undermine the ability of the gymnast to learn the more advanced skills that develop from it.

The Prerequisite Sub-Skills

In order to teach the handstand with good technique the gymnast must first possess the following attributes: good straight body posture, full range of movement in the shoulder joint and good core strength to be able to control the mid-body.

Core Strength

The exercises shown will help to develop the mid body strength required to control mid-body stability for the handstand.

Dished shape.

Back arched shape.

Dished shape on elbows.

The gymnast should first learn to take their weight on to their hands by curling, not jumping, into the supported, tucked handstand.

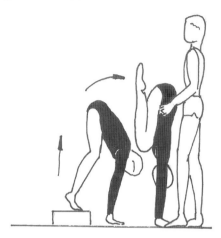

Taking the weight on the arms.

Levering to Handstand

The gymnast should push gently from the bent leg and lever the top or lead leg towards the vertical. The shoulders, hips and heels should arrive in that order into the handstand position. This lever into handstand technique will discourage a kick into the handstand, which tends to result in an arched body.

Levering to handstand.

Once the gymnast can lever slowly into the handstand with correct technique the supported handstand may be held for an increasing period of time. The handstand should be performed with a slightly 'dished to straight' body shape. As the gymnast's strength and awareness improves he or she may progress to light support on the lower legs or hips as shown.

It is good practice to perform the handstand in a variety of situations such as on the floor, on a small balance beam, on floor parallel bars and on a single floor bar.

Coaching the Straddled Lift to Handstand

The straddled lift to handstand is a more advanced skill but it is the foundation for a number of movements on the floor and on other male and female gymnastics apparatus.

The prerequisites include:
- The ability to perform a held handstand as described above but unsupported
- Good flexibility in the hips and shoulders

- The ability to perform the Japana straddled swim round movement, as illustrated and described below.

This flexibility exercise starts in the Japana position, which consists of a seated straddle leg position with the legs at approximately 90 degrees apart and with the chest placed on or close to the floor between the legs. The legs are circled slowly backward through front splits (box splits) to front lying with feet together. During the circling of the legs the hips should remain close to the floor.

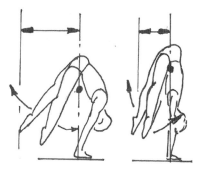

The lever in the straddle to handstand.

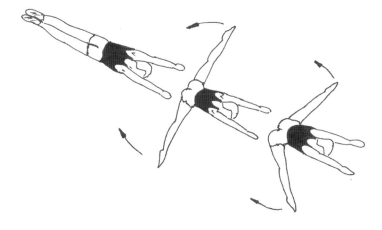

Japana straddled swim round.

This valuable flexibility exercise will enable the straddle lift to handstand to be performed with ease and with good technique since the straddled legs can remain close to the torso throughout the lift. The legs can effectively be circled sideways, whereas if the gymnast does not possess sufficient hip flexibility the legs will move away from the torso and create a much greater lever.

Progressions for Coaching the Straddle Lift

This sub-skill enables the gymnast to learn the important roll of the hips into the vertical while drawing the straddled legs towards the torso in order to minimize the lever created by the legs moving away from the torso.

Supporting the lift to handstand.

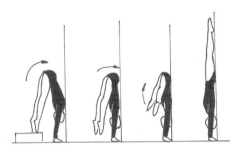

Levering against a wall.

From this position the legs should separate wide to allow them to be circled sideways towards the handstand position.

Once the skill above has been learned with good technique the movement can be performed with support at the hips. The same sideways circling of the legs should be encouraged to minimize the lever, which would otherwise be created if they were allowed to move away from the torso. The amount of support can be reduced gradually as strength and confidence improves.

Straddled Half Lever Lift

As the strength and technique improves the skills shown can be taught. This important skill can be the basis for many others on men's and women's apparatus.

The straddled lever lift to handstand.

CHAPTER 13

COACHING FLOOR EXERCISE SKILLS

The number of gymnastic elements or skills are too numerous to cover in one publication. The author has therefore been selective in order to give a general introduction to the principles and methods used to coach some skills that are important in the movement vocabulary of any gymnast. The floor exercise skills included have been selected since they are fundamental skills that are common to both men's artistic and women's artistic gymnastics.

In artistic gymnastics men and women perform their routines on a sprung and carpeted floor area measuring 12 × 12 metres. The maximum duration for the exercise is 70 seconds for men and 90 seconds for women. The men's floor exercise focuses mainly on a variety of tumbling skills, strength and balance elements.

The women's routines must include tumbling and acrobatic skills linked with leaps and dance skills. The routine is performed to music.

The modern gymnastics facility will usually include a variety of training aids that can help with the coaching of floor skills, and in particular the tumbling skills. Most gyms will have a 12 × 12m sprung and carpeted floor area and some may have trampolines or trampettes (small trampolines) upon which aerial skills can be learned. The advantages of using these rebound apparatuses are that they provide more flight time in order to achieve the skill and also permit many more repetitions before fatigue sets in.

A valuable training aid, the tumble track was developed specifically for training tumble skills and this is a 1.5m wide sprung track approximately 20m long. A foam-filled landing pit or safety mat landing area is normally installed at the end of the tumble track.

More recently a 1.5m wide extended trampoline called a fast track has been introduced to the modern gymnastic facility and this also has a foam-filled pitted landing area at the end.

Recommended use of Training Aids for Tumbling Skills

The following sequence of stages is recommended when teaching the more advanced tumbles such as combinations of somersaults.

*   Introduce the skill movement pattern on floor and safety mats with full support from the coach to ensure the correct technique is understood
*   The trampoline with overhead supporting rig or a trampette on to safety landing mats may be used with care to develop spatial awareness
*   The fast track may then be used to link the tumbles
*   The tumble track is used to more closely link the amount of spring to that of the floor area

- The tumble or tumbling combination is then transferred to the floor with the landing terminating on to safety mats
- Finally, the skills can then be performed on the floor area with landings being executed directly on to the floor.

At each stage of progression the coach should provide a suitable level of physical support to ensure the safety of the gymnast and to ensure the correct technique is learned. Only when each stage of progression can be performed consistently with confidence and correct technique should the level of support be reduced progressively.

Coaching the Cartwheel

The cartwheel is a basic skill that is rarely seen in modern routines but it is still a very useful skill to teach to young gymnasts. It will provide the young gymnast with co-ordination skills, body alignment awareness and experience in sequencing of arm and leg movements.

The Technique for the Cartwheel

The entry into the cartwheel may be sideways but it is more useful to teach it from a forward facing entry since there is a direct relationship with the handstand. If the gymnast naturally leads with the left leg into a handstand then it is recommended the same (left) leg leads into the cartwheel.

1. The coach should stand ahead and to the side of the gymnast so the gymnast's back will be facing the coach. In a left leg cartwheel the coach stands to the left of the gymnast as this will avoid the legs colliding with the coach. This is shown in the illustration above
2. The gymnast steps forward into a lunge position with the shoulder and arm angle remaining open. The coach should lean sideways to place the nearest hand on the gymnast's waist while the second hand crosses over to be placed upon the trailing hip at the waist. The gymnast makes a quarter turn, placing the first hand close to the lead foot
3. The gymnast swings the second leg (right)

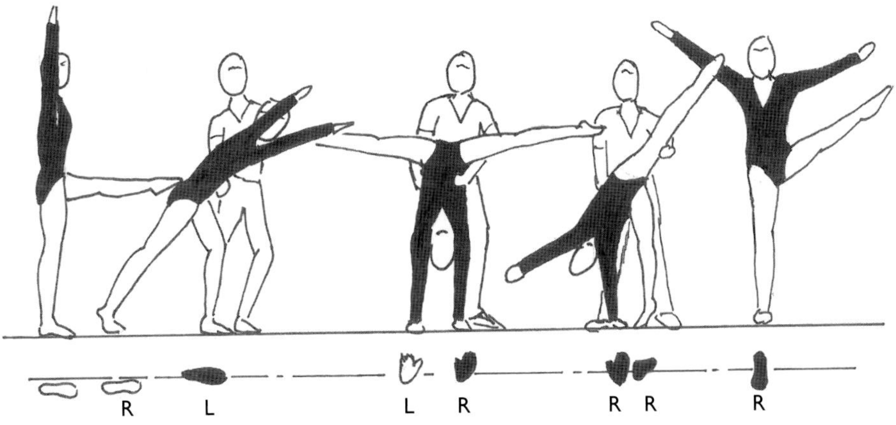

Supporting the cartwheel.

into straddled momentary handstand while the coach supports at the waist. The gymnast's hands should be at 90 degrees to the line of travel

4. The gymnast's lead leg (right) is lowered to the floor and is placed close to the second hand and the lead hand pushes against the floor to raise the torso

5. The gymnast is encouraged to press through the support leg while drawing the torso upward towards the vertical position. If the gymnast has sufficient range of movement in the hips (side splits) the coach can reposition the left hand under the upper leg to hold the leg high as the torso is raised. This will give an elegant position before the leg is lowered to the side to finish in a sideways standing position.

The prerequisites: Before teaching the cartwheel it is important to teach progressive weight bearing on the hands such a those used in the development of the handstand.

The Cartwheel with a Quarter Turn Inwards

Once the cartwheel has been learned successfully variations such as the forward entry cartwheel, one-handed cartwheel and differing exits can be experimented with. It is recommended that one particularly useful exit from the cartwheel, the quarter turn inwards, is learned since this is a useful progression for the round off skill.

The Technique for the Cartwheel Quarter Turn Inwards

1. As the gymnast exits from the cartwheel the gymnast presses through the standing leg and, while lifting the arms and torso upward, the torso begins to turn inwards

2. The second leg is brought alongside the lead leg to complete the quarter turn to face the opposite direction.

The cartwheel with quarter turn inwards.

Coaching the Snap Up Action

The importance of teaching the snap up or courbette action cannot be overemphasized. This action involves making a rapid change in the shape of a handstand from 'arch' to 'dish' while introducing a strong 'snap upward' of the torso to bring the feet in to the floor and the shoulders quickly upward and backward. This action is used extensively in such skills as the round off, back flip and in Tsukahara and Yurchenko-based vaults.

The 'Snap Up' action.

The Technique for the Snap Up

The movement starts in a slightly hollow back 'arched' handstand.

A short sharp kick downwards of the feet into a slightly 'dished' body shape creates an equal and opposite reaction force on the hands. This is accompanied by a strong thrust through the arms and shoulders.

The reaction from the hands lifts the arms and shoulders and, since the body is now in flight, it will begin to rotate about the centre of mass. A tight, dished body shape will result in the feet rotating forward and downward towards the floor while the shoulders and torso rotate upward and backward.

The feet should arrive at the floor beneath the centre of mass and upon landing the body should continue to rotate backward about the feet.

Coaching Progressions for the Snap Up

Prior to teaching the snap up the gymnast must possess good strength when flexing the shoulders and arms and must have good mid-body core strength and the ability to change the body shape rapidly from an 'arched' into a 'dished' shape.

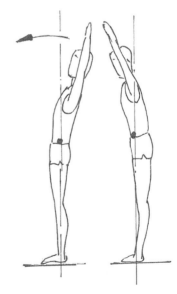

Arch to dish body shapes.

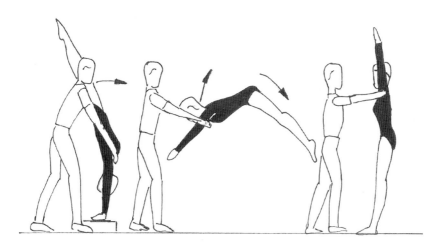

Assisted snap up (1).

In the first of these two assisted snap up drills:

- The coach supports under the armpits with the gymnast's legs resting on the coach's shoulder
- The coach initiates the snap of the legs by pushing with the shoulder, then pulls instantly with the arms to elevate the shoulders
- The coach rotates the shoulders upward and backward to bring the feet downward and forward to end in an off balance standing position
- At the point of landing on the feet the coach must retain a firm hold of the arms to rest the backward rotation.

In the second assisted snap up the coach supports high on the front of the chest with the near hand and on the back of the lower leg with the second hand. The coach lifts and rotates the gymnast into the correct positions, as described above.

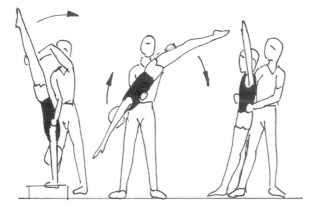

Assisted snap up (2).

Coaching the Round Off

The round off (RO) is a very important floor skill since it is used frequently to convert momentum in a forward direction into a backward direction. It is often referred to as an 'accelerator' since the transfer of momentum can be speeded up if the RO is performed correctly.

The prerequisites: A cartwheel with quarter turn inwards performed with good alignment and good technique, and an ability to perform a rapid and strong snap up from the hands.

Teaching Progressions for the RO

Progression one: Rehearse the snap up and the cartwheel with quarter turn inwards, encouraging a rapid lift of the torso and snapping the legs down towards the floor in the flight from the hands to the feet.

Progression two: Introduce the RO from a low platform to enable the gymnast to experience the push from the arms and the upward and backward lift in the shoulders. The slight increase in flight will enable the gymnast to feel and understand the rotation about the c of m as the torso lifts and the feet descend.

Progression three: Introduce pre-jump into the RO to increase the forward momentum into it. During the jump the tension in the body should be retained, the legs split slightly with the rear leg being placed behind the c of m. Upon landing on the rear leg, the leading front leg steps into

Round off from a platform.

the lunge position. The reaction from landing on the back leg creates a reaction force that forces the torso forward. The chest and arms should be driven forward and downward towards the floor. The leading hand should be rotated to point slightly towards the leading foot and the second hand should be rotated in the same direction and placed on the floor. The alignment between the first and second hand should be at least in line but preferably outside the line of travel. This will facilitate a strong push into the snap up from the arms and shoulders.

Alignment of the round off.

It is important to ensure the feet and shoulders are in correct alignment as the RO is completed to ensure the entry into the following movement is 'square on'.

Progression four: A run-up of up to three steps can be added to the entry into the RO to gain an optimum level of momentum into and out of it.

It is important the gymnast gains experience in adjusting the position of the feet in relation to the c of m on the exit from the RO as this is governed by the trajectory of flight and rotation of the movement that is to follow the skill.

Round Off into Straight Body Jump

The RO of should be performed with control and should land with the feet behind the c of m. This will enable the backward momentum to be arrested and the jump to be executed without rotation.

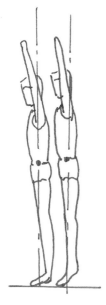

Position of c of m at take-off for straight jump.

Round Off into a Backward Somersault

The RO should land with the feet slightly backward of the c of m to enable the immediate thrust from the legs to lift the c of m upward into the required trajectory and to enable a turning effect to be created.

Take-off for back somersault.

Round Off into a Back Flip

The exit from the round off should be with the feet slightly in front of the c of m to enable

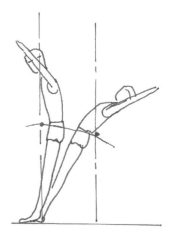

Take-off for back flip.

the backward momentum to be maintained and a low trajectory to be established.

Coaching the Backward Roll to Handstand

There are a number of gymnastic skills that require the gymnast to open the angle between the arms and the shoulders rapidly while simultaneously retaining the mid-body tension. The backward roll to handstand on floor is an excellent means of teaching the gymnast this powerful action prior to the skill being introduced on other pieces of gymnastic apparatus.

Backward roll down incline.

The prerequisites:
The gym-nast should be able to perform the basic backward roll and a good stable handstand before the progressions for the backward roll to handstand are introduced.

Tucked backward roll.

The Backward Roll

When using the progressions shown above to develop the backward role it is important to reduce the load on the head and neck by pushing through the arms to elevate the hips. This will also enable the feet to be brought forward underneath the hips to finish in the squat position.

Straight Leg Backward Roll to Front Support

To perform this progression the gymnast must have sufficient range of movement in the hamstrings and lower back to permit the deep fold of the body in the entry.

The gymnast must bend at the hips with the chest moving towards the thighs and reach backward with the arms to the floor with the fingers pointing forward. The downward momentum is controlled by bending arms. Once the seat contacts the floor, the arms are taken quickly backward at shoulder width apart and the hands are rotated inward to protect the wrists. As the hips pass the point directly over the head, a press through the arms and shoulders elevates the hips and the feet are directed downwards into the front support position.

Straight leg backward roll.

Strengthening the Shoulder Extension

The exercise uses elastic strands to develop the action and strength to open the angle between the arms and shoulders vigorously while retaining the tension in the mid-body. The exercise should be performed as three

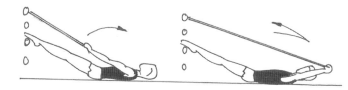

Elastic strand strength exercise.

sets of eight to ten repetitions and the resistance increased gradually as the strength improves.

The Backward Roll to Handstand with Straight Arms

This skill commences with a deep fold of the body and roll backward with straight legs. Once the seat and lower back touch the floor the arms are quickly moved backward to contact the floor with the hands rotated inward. The torso and legs continue to rotate backward and at the point when the feet are directly above the eyes the gymnast presses downward through the hands and arms. This will force the shoulder angle to open and cause the feet to rise through a vertical line above the head.

The body must remain tensioned as it extends into the dished handstand position. The arms and hands should continue to press against the floor as the legs are piked down to the floor.

Backward roll to handstand.

Coaching the Handspring

The prerequisites: These include a competent handstand with strong mid-body control, an ability to perform a handstand forward roll, a high degree of shoulder support strength and good landing technique.

Handspring from a platform.

Coaching Progressions

After first checking the quality of the handstand the gymnast may perform the handspring from a low platform to enable him or her to experience the flight from the hands to the feet. The coach should provide support initially to the side and just ahead of the gymnast, supporting with the nearest hand under the shoulder and with the second hand being placed under the thighs. As the gymnast drives the lead leg powerfully through the handstand position, and thrusts from the arms, the coach must lift the gymnast through the correct flight path. The coach should remain in contact with the gymnast until the landing has been achieved successfully.

matted surface. The technique should be as follows:

1. The leading leg drive should be controlled so as to not pass through the handstand
2. As the legs are brought together a powerful arm and shoulder thrust is introduced
3. This should occur just prior to the handstand and should be sufficient to create the hop on to the higher surface
4. On the completion of the hop the feet should be lowered to the floor but if the gymnast passes beyond the handstand he or she should be prepared to roll out of it.

Developing the Shoulder Thrust

Before attempting to perform the handspring on the floor it is important for the gymnast to become proficient in thrusting from the arms and shoulders. This can be achieved by performing 'handstand hops' from one matted surface to a slightly higher

Handstand hops.

Supporting the handspring.

Assisted Handspring on the Floor

The initial attempts should be supported by the coach standing to the side and ahead of the gymnast and supporting with the near hand under the shoulder and the second hand across the back of the thighs. The gymnast should enter the handspring from a jump or short run-up to gain some forward momentum. The amount of support can be reduced gradually or the support transferred to the waist and then eventually to shadowing the performance.

Key Coaching Points for the Handspring

1. The exit from the pre-jump should land on the rear leg before stepping into the lunge. This will cause a reaction from the floor to propel the gymnast forward
2. The gymnast should drive the chest downwards towards the floor while keeping the shoulder angle open
3. Once the hands are placed on the floor the rear leg should be driven powerfully towards the handstand position
4. This is followed immediately by straightening the front leg and then accompanied by the thrust from the arms and extension from the shoulders

5. The c of m will now follow a parabolic flight path and the body will rotate about it while in flight
6. The head position should remain neutral throughout the performance and the arms should remain parallel above the head during the flight
7. Upon contacting with the feet on the floor the forward rotation and downward momentum can be controlled or used according to the skill that will follow the handspring as follows:

A: When performed as a single skill the landing should be with the feet in front of the c of m so a counter-force can be created against the floor to arrest the forward rotation and the downward momentum should be absorbed by controlled flexing of the hips, knees and ankles while forcing the arms downward simultaneously.

B: When the following skill requires a rebound jump and forward rotation, the feet should land almost directly under the c of m. This enables a rapid rebound force from the legs to be exerted while the c of m pivots about the feet. This is accompanied by dishing the body and the arms driving upward and forward. These actions combine to add to the height and direction of the flight path of the c of m and degree of angular momentum at the point of take-off (rotation).

C: If the intention of the handspring is to generate maximum forward momentum, such as when adding a fly spring to the combination, then the feet should land slightly behind the c of m. This will ensure the forward momentum and required low flight path of the c of m is maintained and the reaction from the floor will increase the amount of forward rotation.

Coaching the Back Flip

The back flip is a very important 'backward accelerator' skill that is used to develop the backward momentum required for entry into the many backward take-off skills such as backward somersaults, which are performed frequently in the tucked, piked or stretched body shape. The back flip is often preceded by a round off in order to maximize the generation of backward momentum.

The prerequisites: A strong handstand shape with good mid-body tension, strong arm and shoulder support strength, an ability to change body shape rapidly from arch to dish and a good understanding and ability to perform a powerful snap up from the handstand position.

Coaching Progressions for the Back Flip

Entry into the Back Flip
The technique for entry is critical for a successful performance and the essential points are:
1. From the standing position the gymnast must lower the arms forward while forcing the seat backward into an off balance dished shape to create the initial backward movement
2. The gymnast should then bend at the knees, ensuring the heels remain on the floor and the knees move behind the feet. The arms are lowered to approximately waist height
3. The legs are then straightened, followed immediately by the extension of the body.
4. It is essential the knees do not move forward in front of the feet during this phase of the leg thrust. It is also important the heels remain firmly in contact with the floor
5. The powerful drive of the arms is introduced just as the leg thrust and stretching of the body is nearing completion. The combined effect of the off-centre leg thrust and the arm drive produces the required backward trajectory of the c of m. The flight path should be in a backward direction in a parabolic curve reaching just above waist height at its highest point
6. In this progression it is safer for the gymnast to be supported by the coach to ensure the correct feel and understanding is achieved and the movement can be performed to land in a flat back or slight dish shape on inclined safety mats as shown.

Entry into the back flip.

The Snap Up from Handstand

Before the full shape of the back flip is attempted it is recommended the snap up from handstand is rehearsed as this will remove a lot of anxiety since the gymnast will already be aware of how to exit the back flip safely.

Ensure the gymnast snaps the feet vigorously into a dished shape and snaps the shoulders and torso upward and backward to rotate the feet into the floor.

Slow Rehearsal of the Whole Pattern of Movement

In this progression the coach stands behind and to the side of the gymnast and supports with the near hand behind the thighs and the second hand behind the lower back. Remember that the gymnast must travel backward during the flight so the coach must be alert to the required flight path. The gymnast is encouraged to produce the correct movements slowly and with correct technique as the coach 'shapes' him or her through the required movement pattern. It should be noted that:

The flight from the feet on to the hands should travel a distance equivalent to the length of the gymnast's legs and torso combined

The flight from the hands to the feet will vary but should be between zero and 35cm.

The snap up action.

The hands should be either pointing forward or preferably rotated slightly inward when placed on the floor.

The Common Errors in the Back Flip

The most common errors occur at the beginning of the back flip and these are illustrated below.

Knees Moving Forward

If the gymnast remains on balance and his or her knees are allowed to move forward the heels will come off the floor. This results in a lack of leg thrust and the gymnast will

Supporting and shaping the back flip.

tend to travel forward and with insufficient flight. This may cause the gymnast to land on his or her back, or worse on his or her neck.

Driving the arms too early.

Forward movement of the knees.

Driving the Arms too Early

The gymnast may give the appearance they are leaning off balance but if he or she drives the arms upward and backward before the leg thrust is completed, it may result in the flight path being too high and with insufficient backward rotation being generated.

The Complete Back Flip

Once the pattern of movement is understood fully and executed consistently the gymnast should be encouraged to exert more speed and power into the movement.

This should be done with full physical support from the coach during the early learning stages and he or she must be alert continually to the possibility of erroneous attempts.

As the quality and consistency improves the coach may reduce gradually the degree of physical support.

The round off may then precede the back flip to increase the backward momentum but the coach is advised to support the back flip during the initial attempts at this combination and continue to do so until competence and consistency is proven.

The round off back flip.

Exiting from the Back Flip

As with other accelerator skills, positioning the feet upon exiting the back flip can be varied to accommodate the required take-off and flight path of the skill to follow. These variations are illustrated above and described below:

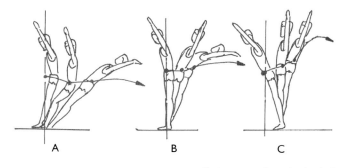

Various exits from the back flip.

A: If the back flip is to be followed by another back flip the feet should be brought just in front of the c of m to ensure the entry into the second back flip is off balance and the trajectory is about waist high.

B: When the back flip precedes a whip back salto the feet should exit the back flip almost directly under the c of m in order to maintain the backward momentum. This permits a slight elevation of the c of m into the flight trajectory at around mid-chest height.

C: When it is intended to perform a backward somersault following the back flip the exit from the back flip should be with the feet behind the c of m. This permits a strong thrust from the legs to elevate the c of m into a higher flight path at around shoulder height.

Key Coaching Points for the Back Flip
- Commence from an off balance position, momentarily falling backward
- When bending the hips and knees ensure the knees remain behind the feet
- During the leg thrust the heels should remain on the floor
- The leg thrust and extension of the mid-body should be in unison and followed immediately by the drive of the arms
- The initial flight path of the c of m should be just above waist height and travel the length of the gymnast's body
- The snap up should cause the body to rotate rapidly about the c of m to lift the shoulders and to bring the feet forward into the floor
- The flight length from the hands to feet should be relatively short.

Coaching the Backward Somersault

The natural progression from the round off back flip is the backward somersault (BS) since this skill can use the backward momentum generated from these backward accelerators. The backward somersault can be performed in the tucked, piked or stretched body shape. Once the BS has been mastered it can be developed to include a number of twists and/or performed with more than a single rotation as in the double backward somersault.

The prerequisites:
- Consistent and correct performance of an RO back flip
- A good understanding of the change of shape from stretched body into a tuck, then into the stretched shape again

- Ability to perform a backward roll as a safe outlet upon landing
- Good understanding and correct landing technique when landing backward
- Appropriate level of physical preparation of the legs and mid-body.

Understanding the Factors that Affect Rotation

It is much easier to rotate the body in a tucked shape than in the stretched body shape due to the lower resistance to rotation of the reduced body shape. This is because the distribution of the body's mass is closer to the point of rotation (the c of m) in the tucked shape. This measurement is called the 'moment of inertia' and is a measure of the resistance of the body to rotation in the particular body shape.

A: The Tucked Shape

The body mass is distributed close to the c of m and therefore the resistance to rotation is smaller.

B: The Stretched Shape

The body mass is distributed further away from the c of m, therefore the lever is longer and the resistance to rotation is greater.

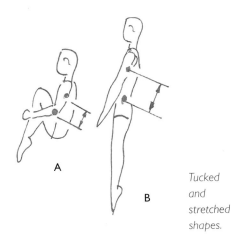

A

B

Tucked and stretched shapes.

The consequence of the different resistances to rotation of the body shapes means the gymnast needs to generate much greater amounts of rotation to rotate in the stretched body shape than when the body is in the tucked shape.

It must be noted, however, that when the gymnast enters the backward somersault from the back flip the initial take-off must be in the stretched body shape. This is due to the fact that when the body is stretched it can use the backward momentum to create maximum angular momentum (the degree rotation) while the feet are in contact with the floor. You should encourage the gymnast to raise his or her arms during take-off to maximize this effect.

The take-off will also determine the height and trajectory of the flight path of the c of mass and these will be influenced by the position of the c of m in relation to the feet and the amount of force added through the leg thrust and arm lift. It should also be noted that during the 'take-off' phase the body will pivot (rotate) about the feet.

Once the feet have left the floor the amount of rotation and the flight path of the c of m is fixed and can no longer be influenced by the gymnast. When in flight the body will rotate about the c of m and a change in body shape, i.e. lowering the arms or adopting the tucked shape, will reduce the resistance to rotation and its speed will increase. Similarly, if the body is then extended (stretched) the speed of rotation will be reduced due to the greater resistance to rotation. However, the body will still possess the same amount of angular momentum as when first taking off.

This factor is important since it influences what the gymnast must do to control the landing. When preparing for the landing he or she must stretch the body and extend the legs and lift the arms to slow down the speed of rotation. When contacting the floor the arms should press downward and forward and bending the hips, knees and ankles should be controlled to arrest the backward momentum.

Key points Influencing the Take-Off Technique

- Lift the arms and extend the body at take-off to maximize the generation of angular momentum
- The height and trajectory of the flight path of the c of m will be determined by:
  1. The position of the c of m in relation to the feet at take-off
  2. The amount of force gained from the leg thrust and arm lift
- The body will pivot around the feet during the take-off and will rotate around the c of m when in flight
- Immediately after take-off the arms should be lowered quickly to reduce the resistance and to speed up rotation
- In preparation for the landing the body and legs should be extended and the arms lifted
- Upon landing controlled bending of the hips, knees and ankles will be used to absorb and arrest the backward momentum.

Coaching Progressions for the Tucked Backward Somersault

Having first discussed and explained the key points of the take-off, the creation of the flight path, the control of somersault rotation and the correct technique for the landing the coaching of the backward somersault may begin.

The Tucked Backward Somersault

Progression one: With the gymnast lying on the back on the floor with the arms by the side introduce the sequence of:

1. Lift the arms above the head at shoulder width apart to simulate the take-off
2. Simultaneously snap the arms forward and downwards and rapidly change the body into a tuck shape
3. Simulate the preparation for landing by extending the body and legs and lifting the arms.

Progression two: Teach the basic standing tucked back somersault from a suitable platform. This will provide more flight time for the gymnast to gain experience in performing the sequence of movements and enable them to adjust to landing with backward momentum. This progression should be performed with support from the coach.

Tuck back somersault from a platform.

After rehearsing the round off back flip and ensuring a consistent point of take-off, the following sequence of progressions can be introduced but remember to allow time for the Three Cs (Consolidation, Consistency and Confidence) to be experienced.

Back flip stretched jump BS.

RO Back flip three-quarter tucked.

RO Back Flip Tucked
Backward Somersault

The coach should support the gymnast initially to ensure the correct technique and flight path are created and to ensure his or her safety.

Once the point of take-off has been established the coach should stand behind and to the side of the gymnast and support the take-off, somersault and landing. There are a number of recommended methods of support, which may include:

• Nearest hand behind the thighs, second hand on middle of the back to create lift and direction at take-off, release the contact, then support near hand under the chest and second hand behind the upper back for controlled landing
• Nearest hand on lower back second hand on front of torso at take-off, remain in contact and arms cross to support landing.
• As the gymnast progresses the support may be reduced gradually through various stages: full support, light support and shadowing then supporting the landing.

The round off back flip tucked back somersault.

Coaching the Stretched Backward Somersault

Progression one: Once the round off back flip tucked backward somersault has been mastered successfully the stretched backward somersault may be developed. Again the first step is to determine the take-off point after the RO back flip and then add a stretched jump to the preliminary sequence. The coach must provide adequate support to prevent the gymnast from over-rotating in the jump.

Progression two: The jump can be performed in the situation shown with the first stage being to land on the shoulders on the platform with the hands raised above the head to protect the neck.

Progression three: Once this progression can be performed safely the gymnast can be supported through a three-quarter stretched back somersault to land on the platform of safety mats on his or her front with the arms and full body absorbing the impact.

The Round off Back Flip Stretched Backward Somersault

The full sequence can be introduced as the final stage with the support from the coach

Stretched three-quarter somersault.

being reduced gradually as the gymnast's technique and confidence grows.

The Key Coaching Points for the Stretched Backward Somersault

- Ensure the round off back flip is consistent and technically correct
- At the exit from the back flip the feet should be slightly behind the c of mass
- At the take-off the arms must lift up quickly as the legs provide the thrust and the hips must push slightly forward and upward causing the chest to lift and the shoulders to move slightly backward behind the c of m
- On completion of the take-off the arms must be driven rapidly forward and downward towards the thighs to reduce the resistance to rotation
- A straight to slightly arched body shape should be maintained throughout the somersault and the head should remain neutral

The round off back flip stretched back somersault.

- To prepare for the landing the arms should be lifted above the head to slow down the speed of rotation
- On landing the feet should be slightly behind the c of m and controlled bending of the hips, knees and ankles should absorb and arrest the backward momentum
- The arms may be circled backward to help control the rotation on landing.

Adding a Full Twist to the Stretched Backward Somersault

Once the stretched backward somersault can be performed consistently with good technique, adding a twist may be a useful progression. Please refer to the section on twisting with backward rotation in the section on biomechanics.

The first stage is to introduce a half twist in to the somersault. After the take-off has been completed and the gymnast is in flight a simple sideways displacement of one arm or drop of a shoulder is sufficient to create a half twist. Introducing a half twist in the first instance will allow the gymnast to experience the effect of the twist and will facilitate the development of orientation and spatial awareness. The coach should shadow the initial attempts to ensure a safe landing is achieved.

When the gymnast is confident and competent at performing the half twist the full twist may then be developed. It is recommended the initial attempts are supported fully and the landing should be firstly into a landing pit and then progressed to a safety mat.

The most efficient technique involves the gymnast producing a high somersault with the body aligned square at take-off and with a slight arch in the body shape. The backward arched shape allows a hula twist action to assist the creation of the twist. Immediately the feet leave the floor the left arm should be forced rapidly backward and downward to the left side. This instills a tilt twist to the left into the body and once the action is started both arms should be 'wrapped' close to the body to accelerate the twist. The gymnast should aim to complete the twist at around the top of the flight path.

After completing the twist the arms should be opened and raised above the head to reduce the twist rotation and somersault rotation respectively in preparation for the landing. It is possible to introduce the twist as a 'torque twist' while the feet are in contact with the floor. However, this is only necessary if multiple twists are to be introduced and torque twisting should be discouraged for the half and full twist.

Back somersault with full twist.

Coaching the Forward Somersault

The forward somersault may be performed in the tucked, piked or stretched body shape and carried out with or without twists. As with the backward somersault, it is easier to perform the forward somersault in the tucked shape since the resistance to rotation is less. The forward somersault may be performed as a single element but it is more usual to perform it in combination with other skills. It may be performed from a short run-up but is frequently preceded by either a handspring or a two-footed take-off handspring (fly spring).

The prerequisites: The ability to perform successfully and accurately:

- a short run-up into a hurdle step and stretched jump
- a dive forward roll
- a controlled landing from a forward jump from a raised platform.

Coaching Progressions for a Tucked Forward Somersault

Once the prerequisites listed above have been rehearsed and checked for competent performance then the following sequence of progressive stages may be introduced to teach the tucked forward somersault.

Progression one: Dive forward roll on to a platform of safety mattresses. From a short run-up and hurdle step the gymnast should place the feet slightly in front of the c of m and as the arms are driven upward and forward the thrust from the legs is added. The body should be dished slightly as the feet leave the floor into the flighted phase. The coach should provide support in the initial attempts to control the direction of flight at take-off and to regulate the degree of forward rotation.

The support is provided with the near hand on the front of the thighs just above the knees and the second hand is placed upon the front of the torso just below the rib cage.

Progression two: The front somersault tucked may then be introduced with the coach providing full support from the point of the take-off through to the controlled landing.

From the run-up and pre-jump the gymnast should again place the feet just ahead of the c of m and with the arms stretched upward to create a large turning moment about the feet. This allows the feet to press forward against the floor to create an equal and opposite reaction force from the floor that adds

The dive forward roll.

to large turning moment as the body pivots about the feet. This produces the maximum angular momentum (rotation) at the point of take-off. As the arms are driven forward and upward, the body shape should be changed to a dished shape at the same time as the leg thrust is imparted to the body.

At this point the height and trajectory of the flight path of the c of m and the amount of angular momentum has been created. As soon as the feet leave the floor the arm should be taken rapidly downward and forward as the hips and legs adopt the tucked shape quickly. This reduces the resistance to rotation and the speed of rotation increases.

The hands should clasp the shins to hold the tight tuck of the body. After approximately three-quarters of the somersault has been completed the gymnast should begin to lift the arms upward and extend at the hips and legs. This will increase the resistance to rotation to slow down its speed in preparation for the landing.

Upon landing the feet should arrive at the floor slightly in front of the c of m to enable a counter-force to be used to arrest forward the rotation. The hips, ankles and knees are flexed with controlled force to absorb the forward and downward momentum.

The arms should be forced downward and forward to reduce the impact of the landing on the body.

Supporting the Tucked Front Somersault

The coach should provide full support in the learning stages as described below.

Standing to the side and ahead of the gymnast at the point of take-off, the nearest hand is rotated outwards and placed across the stomach of the gymnast. The second hand reaches behind the gymnast and is placed on the upper torso. This method of support allows the coach to dictate the height and direction of flight and to also regulate the degree of rotation. As the gymnast extends the body and legs in preparation for the landing the coach should remove the near hand quickly from the stomach and grasp the forearm of the gymnast's nearest arm as it is raised above the head. This relocation of the support to the arm is essential as it will enable the coach to control the rotation more easily upon landing and avoid the risk of the gymnast over-rotating. The grasp on the arm should be retained until the gymnast has come to rest.

Coaching the Stretched Forward Somersault

Once the tucked forward somersault has been mastered successfully and a period of consolidation permitted the gymnast may

Supporting the front somersault.

Three-quarter stretched front somersault.

proceed to learning the piked, or more importantly the stretched, forward somersault. The first stage is to develop the strength and technique to generate sufficient angular momentum at take-off. This can be achieved by introducing a stretched three-quarter somersault on to a platform of safety mats as illustrated below.

Following the run-up and pre-jump the feet position and take-off should be similar to that described for the tucked front somersault. However, the technique for the drive of the arms is distinctly different. At the point of take-off the body should assume a slightly dished shape and the arms are driven forward initially at just above shoulder height to create the appropriate flight path of the c of m. As the feet leave the floor the arms should move quickly sideways at shoulder height to reduce rapidly the resistance to rotation. During flight the body should retain a tensioned slight dish or stretched shape and just prior to landing on the back the arms should be brought above the head.

The coach should provide support during the early learning stages to ensure the safety of the gymnast and to enable him or her to feel the correct technique. The coach should stand to the side and forward of the gymnast at the point of take-off and support him or her with the near hand on the front of the

thighs just above the knees and with the second hand supporting on the front of the torso just below the rib cage.

The Stretched Front Somersault
The technique:

- **Pre-jump:** This should be low with the feet arriving on the floor just ahead of the c of m. The arms are above the head with shoulder angle open
- **Take-off:** The arms drive forward at shoulder height and the body should be slightly dished. The feet push forward against the floor to produce an indirect backward turning effect on the feet. The downward thrust of the legs will create the lift and add to the rotation, and the flight path will be determined
- **Somersault phase:** Once the feet leave the floor the heels should lift and the arms should drive sideways at shoulder height or just below this height. This quickly reduces the resistance to rotation and the speed of rotation will increase. The body shape may vary from slightly arched, stretched or slightly dished depending on preference
- **Preparation for landing:** The arms must be raised above the head to increase the resistance to rotation to slow down the speed of rotation

The stretched front
somersault.

- **The landing:** Upon the feet touching the floor the hips, knees and ankles bend with control and the arms are pressed downwards to absorb the momentum.

Providing physical support: The coach can provide support in the initial attempts by standing ahead and to the side of the gymnast at take-off. The nearest hand is placed on the stomach and the second hand is placed on the upper back to guide the take-off and control the degree of rotation. After the take-off, the coach releases the contact with the gymnast and supports him or her on the front and back of the torso to regulate the rotation for landing.

The **exit** from the stretched forward somersault (SFS) will be varied depending on what is the next skill in the combination.

A: Controlled Landing

If the SFS is to be performed as a single skill

with controlled landing the feet should land in front of the c of m.

B: Take-off into Another Somersault

The feet should land just slightly in front of the c of m to allow for the change in body shape into the take-off. The arms are able to drive upward and forward into the take-off into the second somersault.

Take-off into
a second
somersault.

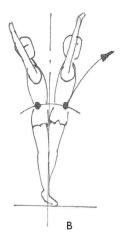

B

A

Controlled landing.

C: Entry into a Tempo-Forward Somersault

If the somersaults are to performed as a combination of fast rotating tempo somersaults the feet should land behind the c of m to project the flight path forward at just above waist height.

Entry into a tempo somersault.

C

Key Coaching Points for the Stretched Front Somersault

The key to success in the SFS is in consistency in the take-off and having sufficient forward and angular momentum at the point of take-off.

Adding a Twist to the Stretched Forward Somersault

When the gymnast can perform the stretched front somersault consistently with good technique a half or full twist may be added. The body alignment should be square at take-off and the twist is introduced as a 'tilt twist' once the feet lose contact with the floor. If the right arm and shoulder are dropped to the right side it will initiate an anticlockwise twist to the left. A half twist should be introduced first to ensure the correct technique can be adopted and to permit familiarity to be gained. This can then be progressed to a full twist by introducing a more vigorous dropping of the arm.

The entrance into the somersault at take-off should be with a slightly dished shape to enable a hula twisting action to aid the tilt twist.

Once the first arm has initiated the twist the second arm should be drawn rapidly across the body to accelerate the twist rotation. Once the twist is completed the arms should be opened wide to reduce the twist velocity and lifted to control the somersault rotation in preparation for the landing.

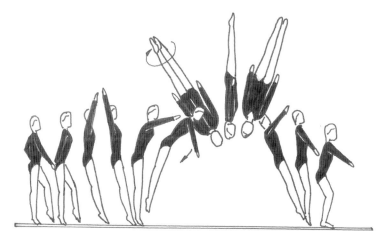

Stretched front somersault with full twist.

CHAPTER 14

COACHING VAULT

The Modern Vaulting Table

Currently the same vaulting table is used for men's and women's gymnastics and the only difference in the apparatus is the height of the table. The men vault at a height of 135cm and the women at 120cm.

The run-up consists of a 25m long, carpeted

Amy Tinkler on the vault.

track together with a sprung take-off board. The landing area is a shock absorbent matted surface of 20cm depth, 6m long and 2.5m wide. The landing surface is marked with a landing zone, which starts at 95cm from the vaulting table and ends at 150cm from it at the end of the landing zone. The purpose of this landing zone is to provide the judges with an accurate indication of the alignment of each vault upon landing.

The Run-up and Take-off for Vaulting

The run-up, pre-jump and take-off are very important features of successful vaulting.

The run-up: This consists of a measured and controlled run that must arrive on the springboard at an optimum horizontal velocity appropriate to the vault being performed.

The pre-jump: Just prior to arriving at the board a hurdle step is performed from the front leg to land with two feet together on the board. The pre-jump on to the board must be performed with a low trajectory to maintain the forward momentum. The arms circle to the rear during the flight and the feet should arrive on the board in front of the c of m.

The action of the pre-jump then depresses the board and the gymnast must co-ordinate the timing of the take-off with the recoil from the board.

The vault take-off.

The take-off: The arms drive upward and forward at around shoulder height as the body pivots about the feet. With the c of m in front of the feet, the leg thrust occurs to lift the c of m into the correct parabolic curve flight path. The reaction from the board sets up the increased rotation of the body that now begins to rotate about the c of m while in flight. It should be noted that the direction of flight of the c of m and the amount of angular momentum (rotation) are determined while in contact with the board and cannot be altered during the flight unless an external force is applied.

Another important point of the take-off is that the velocity of the run-up and the trajectory of the take-off must be adjusted in respect to the type of vault being performed. The length of flight in the pre-flight should be relatively short and the hands should be driven quickly to make contact with the vaulting table so the amount of rotational energy and forward momentum can be maintained.

Key Coaching Points for the Run-up and Take-off
- The length of the run-up should be measured and the acceleration must be gradual
- The velocity (speed) of the run-up is varied according to the type of vault
- Pre-jump should be low and fast to maintain the forward momentum

- The feet must arrive on the board in front of the c of m and the body pivots about the feet on the board
- The arms drive forward at shoulder height to make the contact between the hands and table as quickly as possible.

Coaching Controlled Landings

In addition to practising the landings from the actual vaults, the skill of landing safely and accurately can be reinforced by simulating the landings in both a forward and backward direction. The skill can be enhanced by introducing a twist into the flight before the landing. This requires the gymnast to cope with horizontal momentum, downward forces and rotation about the vertical and horizontal axis of the body.

Key Points for Coaching Forward Facing Landings
- The arms should lift above the shoulders to reduce the rotation
- The feet must be in front of the c of m to enable a counter-turning moment to be created to arrest the forward momentum
- The downward momentum is absorbed by the controlled bending of the hips, the knees and the ankles

- The arms are pressed downward to reduce the downward force on the floor and also opened wide to enable a counter-turning moment to be applied against the floor to arrest the twisting rotation about the vertical axis.

Key Points for Coaching Backward Facing Landings

- The arms are lifted above the head to increase the resistance to rotation to reduce the backward rotation

Forwards landing.

Backwards landings.

Landing forwards with twist.

Landing backwards from twist.

- The feet must be behind the c of m to enable a counter-turning moment to be created to arrest the backward momentum
- The downward force is absorbed by the controlled bending of the hips, the knees and ankles
- Upon landing, the arms are pressed downward to reduce the downward force on the floor and opened wide to counteract the twisting rotation of the body.

General Classification of Vaults

The different types of vaults are categorized according to the direction of entry on to the vaulting platform, as indicated below.

Forward Entry
These include the conventional forward take-off vaults such as the **handspring vault**, which is the basis upon which the more advanced handspring-type vaults are based.

Backward Entry
These vaults require a round off to be performed on to the springboard, together with a backward take-off on to the table. The most common vault in this category is the **Yurchenko vault**.

Round Off Entry
This type of vault uses the conventional forward take-off but requires a quarter turn on to the table so a round off action can be performed on it. This is then followed by a one-and-a-half somersault performed from the thrust of the hands.

Two main vaults that fall into this category are the **Tsukahara vault** and the **Kasamatsu vault**. These are differentiated by the initial direction of somersault rotation from the hands as follows:

In the **Tsukahara vault** the gymnast's chest **faces** the vaulting table after the round off and performs a **backward somersault** from the hands.

In the **Kasamatsu vault** the gymnast makes an additional quarter turn during the round off to face away from the table (i.e. back to the table) and a **forward somersault** is performed from the hands.

The difficulty rating or tariff of each of the vaults can be increased by adding a twist or number of twists or by increasing the number of somersault rotations into the post flight.

Common Vault Coaching Strategies
It is recommended that when coaching each of the core vaults described above the following general strategy is adopted.

- Select a type of vault that suits the gymnast's ability and prowess particularly
- Rehearse the relevant landing drills
- Introduce the run-up, take-off and propulsion from the table into the first phase of the vault to land on a platform of safety mats at table height

IMPORTANT NOTES

- At each stage of progression time must be allocated to consolidate in order to install confidence and consistency
- The coach should reduce the degree of support gradually as the gymnast displays good technique, consistency and confidence with each progression
- The coach should expect a slight underperformance when a new progression is introduced due to anxiety and should be alert and provide the necessary degree of physical support.

- The full vault is then performed to land into a foam-filled landing pit without support from the coach
- The vault is the performed on to safety landing mats placed into the foam landing pit and increased progressively in height until they simulate the height of the competition landing surface
- The vault is then performed, initially with full support, on to a safety mat placed on to the competition landing area
- The depth of the landing surface is reduced gradually to a 10cm landing module placed on the competition landing area.

Coaching the Handspring Vault

The prerequisites: The gymnast must be competent at performing the handspring consistently as a floor exercise skill and possess good strength in the mid-body, arms, shoulders and legs.

Recommended Progressions for Coaching the Handspring Vault

Progression one: Rehearse the run-up, take-off and pre-flight as previously described

Progression two: Practise the handspring landing as shown. Encourage a strong leg

The handspring landing.

drive and thrust from the arms and shoulders to gain rotation and height in the flight. During the flight the arms may be lowered to the side to increase the speed of rotation and raised to reduce the speed of rotation in preparation for the landing.

Progression three – the take-off and propulsion: A powerful but regulated run-up precedes the pre-jump, which should be low and fast.

The arms should circle rearwards during the pre-jump and upon landing on the springboard the feet should be ahead of the c of m and the arms should be behind the body. During contact with the springboard, the arms drive forward and upward as the body pivots about the feet.

The take-off and propulsion.

At the take-off the heels are lifted rearwards and the arms reach forward quickly towards the table. Upon contact with the hands on the table, the body rotates momentarily about the hands as the table stores the energy of the impact from the hands.

As the sprung surface of the vaulting table returns the stored energy to the gymnast's body the shoulder thrust is added. This converts the horizontal forward momentum into vertical lift and at the point where the c of m has moved ahead of the hands a turning moment adds to the forward rotation.

With the gymnast landing on the back it removes the requirement to focus on a controlled landing and this permits him or her to gain experience in the required technique for the main ingredients of the handspring vault.

Progression four: The handspring vault may now be practised in full with the initial attempts being supported by the coach at the take-off (A) supporting with the nearest hand on the front of the thighs and the second hand on the torso just below the ribcage.

The coach should lean towards the gymnast as he or she approaches the take-off and make early contact with the thighs and torso. The coach then guides the gymnast on to the table and adds lift and rotation as required. At this stage the landing is executed on to a safety mat placed on the completion landing area.

A second coach (B) may assist the landing by supporting the front and rear of the torso in order to control the degree of rotation and ensure a secure landing.

As accuracy, consistency and confidence grows, the coach (A) may reduce the amount of support provided at the take-off. The coach should progress to only providing support for the landing or 'shadowing' it to ensure it is achieved safely and accurately.

Key Coaching Points for the Handspring Vault
Ensure that:

- The run-up is measured accurately for each individual gymnast
- Sufficient, controlled run speed is generated
- The flight on to the vaulting table is consistent, the hands drive quickly forward to reach for the table and the heels should be lifted powerfully
- There should be a momentary period while the body pivots around the hands
- The thrust from the hands (the block) should occur just before the body reaches the vertical line and as the energy from the table is returned to the gymnast's body
  - The head should remain neutral throughout
  - The position of the arms can be adjusted to control the degree of rotation
  - During the second flight the body may be either stretched, very slightly dished or slightly arched
  - A controlled landing is executed.

Adding a Twist to the Handspring Vault
Once the handspring vault has been mastered with good technique it is a useful progression to add a half or full twist into the post-flight. It is essential that the post-flight is performed with

The supported handspring vault.

A   B

Handspring with full twist.

sufficient height rather than with high velocity rotation to enable the twist to be completed before the top of the flight is achieved.

The twist is best created as a 'tilt twist' since this is easier to control than a twist initiated as a torque twist in this vault. Please refer to the section on forward somersault rotation and twisting in the biomechanics section.

The twist should be initiated immediately the thrust from the hands is completed. One arm (the right arm in the diagram) is pressed rapidly towards the side of the body. This causes the body axis to tilt and the body will rotate about the longitudinal axis in an anticlockwise direction (twist to the left). The aim is to complete the twist at around the top of the flight curve. The arm should then be raised sideways and upward to reduce the twist rotation and somersault rotation in preparation for the landing.

The head should remain neutral throughout the vault and twist for best effect. It is possible to create the twist from a torque turn produced through the hands against the table surface but this is only recommended if more than a full turn is to be performed.

Coaching the Yurchenko Vault

The Yurckenko vault commences with a controlled run into a round off to land on to the springboard with the back towards the vaulting table. The gymnast then performs a back flip on to the table into one and a half back somersaults from the hands to land on the feet.

The prerequisites: Good strength in the shoulders and arms to create the propulsion from the hands and a high degree of control in the mid-body. The ability to perform a round off back flip into a stretched backward somersault with consistent good technique is a priority.

Recommended Coaching Progressions for the Yurchenko Vault
Progression one: Rehearse the landing from a backward somersault from the vaulting table.

Tuck back somersault landing.

129

Progression two: It is essential the gymnast can arrive consistently on the springboard at the correct point following the round off on to the board.

The starting point for the run-up is best achieved by standing on the springboard at the desired take-off point and then performing the run-up and hurdle step into the round off away from the springboard. The point at which the feet land after the round off is the starting point for the run-up into the vault. The run-up may then be practised on to the board until it is performed consistently.

Progression three: The run-up, round off on to the board together with a take-off to land on the back on a platform of safety mats will permit the gymnast to learn and perfect this combination of skills.

The coach should stand adjacent to the springboard and support him or her with the nearest hand on the back of the thighs and the second hand on the upper back. The coach should guide the flight and control the degree of rotation.

The round off should land high up the board with the feet behind the c of m. The thrust from the legs should occur momentarily before the arm action is added. The gymnast should leave the board in a slightly dished shape and then drive the arms over the head. It is important the head should move backward in unison with the arms and not be thrown independently backward. The landing should be on the shoulders and upper back with the arms overhead and the body in a dished shape.

Progression four: The vaulting table may be introduced once the gymnast can perform the above progression with consistently good technique. This progression allows the gymnast to consolidate the run-up and take-off and to develop an understanding of height and flight of the pre-flight on to the table and the required technique for the thrust from the hands. The flight on to the table should be relatively low with the hand contact with the table occurring with the legs just above the horizontal line of the hips. Upon contact with the table the body will pivot about the hands until it approaches the handstand position. At this point the feet should snap into the dished shape to produce an equal and opposite reaction through the hands against the table. The thrust from the hands occurs simultaneously with this action, causing the lift from the table. The snap up action that was learned previously to perform the round off skill determines the height and flight of the path of the c of m in the post-flight. Once the hands leave the table the body

Round off backward take-off to back landing.

The backward take-off and propulsion from the table.

will rotate about the c of m during the flight from it. The gymnast should retain a tight, dished body shape and raise the arms to reduce the speed of rotation in preparation for the landing.

Progression five: The coach (or coaches) should stand on a suitably stable platform that is at the height of the vaulting table and placed adjacent to the point of contact with the hands on the table. The full vault is performed

Supporting the Yurchenko vault.

with the coach assisting at the point of take-off from the hands on the table. The nearest hand is placed under the front of the torso to assist in the lift of the chest and guide the post-flight path off the table. The second hand is placed behind the knees or thighs to control the somersault rotation.

It is reasonable to permit the gymnast to rotate the somersault in the tucked position for the initial attempts but it is important the snap action is completed fully to generate the required rotation, before the tuck is created.

It is recommended that for heavier gymnasts two coaches should provide the support in this progression.

This should be performed initially to land into a foam landing pit if one is available and progressed gradually through safety mats placed on top of the foam in the landing pit to landing on a safety mat as shown.

Progression six: The final stages require the gymnast to perform the Yurchenko vault on to a safety mat and then on to the competition landing area. This progression should

The Yurchenko vault.

only be introduced once the gymnast is consistent and confident with the previous progressions. Initially support should be provided at the take-off from the springboard and at the landing as shown. This may be reduced gradually to just 'spotting' the landing as confidence and consistency increases.

Key Coaching Points for Coaching the Yurchenko Vault

- Ensure the run-up is measured accurately
- From the round off the feet must land at the apex of the springboard and should be behind the c of m
- Maintain a dished body shape at the take-off, then drive the arms overhead
- Head should remain neutral
- Legs should be level with the height of hips when the hands make contact with the table
- A powerful snap up action occurs just before the handstand position
- Arms must snap downwards towards the thighs to increase rotation
- Retain a slightly dished or stretched body shape throughout the somersault phase.

- Note: The speed of the run-up is usually slightly slower for the Yurchenko vault than that required for other vaults.

Coaching the Tsukahara Vault

The Tsukahara vault comprises a forward take-off from the springboard, a round off on top of the vaulting table to face the table and a one and one half backward somersault executed from the hands.

The prerequisites: Strong arms and shoulders for propulsion from the table; good mid-body control; ability to land successfully from a backward somersault from the vaulting table; the ability to perform round off stretched backward somersault; and a good understanding of the snap up from a round off.

Progressions for Coaching the Tsukahara Vault

Progression one: The gymnast should rehearse the round off on floor on to a safety mat with the emphasis on the powerful snap up and lift of the chest.

Round off over the table to back landing.

Progression two: The landing from a backward somersault performed from a raised platform or the vaulting table should be practised.

Progression three: The next stage is to perform the round off from the vaulting table into a three-quarter stretched backward somersault to land on a platform of safety mats at table height.

The technique requires the gymnast to generate a high degree of forward momentum in the run-up and transfer this quickly into forward rotation from the board.

At the take-off the gymnast must face the table to enable a good heel lift to occur. The hands should reach to make quick contact with the table. The lead hand should be rotated through 90 degrees and as it makes contact with the table the arm should be bent slightly to ensure a thrust from this arm is delayed.

The body then makes a quarter turn to permit the second hand to be placed quickly on to the table, off line to the first hand and with the fingers pointing towards the first hand. This allows a powerful thrust from the arms and shoulders to be introduced with the body aligned correctly with the table.

The Snap Up Action

The thrust from the arms must coincide with the snap of the feet into a dished body shape to generate maximum lift and rotation from the table. The snap of the feet (A) produces an equal and opposite reaction against the table (R). This reaction against the table produces an equal and opposite indirect reaction (IR) from the table. This indirect reaction, together

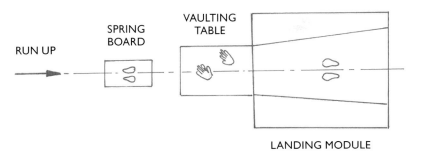

RUN UP

SPRING BOARD

VAULTING TABLE

LANDING MODULE

The correct alignment for the Tsukahara vault.

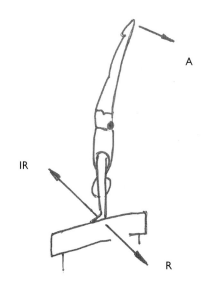

The snap up action.

with the thrust from the arms, lifts the c of m to create the flight path of the c of m and also lifts the shoulders. The indirect reaction force also produces a turning moment about the c of m to increase the angular rotation of the body. As the hands leave the table the arms should be brought forward and downward quickly towards the thighs to reduce the resistance to rotation. This will increase the speed of rotation of the gymnast's body. The

arm should then be raised above the head to slow down the rotation in preparation for landing on the back on the safety mats.

Progression four: The full Tsukahara vault may now be performed over the vaulting table with the initial attempts being performed to land into a foam-filled landing pit if one is available.

The coach should stand on a stable platform to the side of the table and adjacent to the point of arrival of the gymnast in the handstand. The coach must stand to the side so the gymnast's back is to the coach. The nearest hand is placed on the front of the torso on the ribcage to lift the gymnast's chest and the second hand is placed on the rear of the legs to control the rotation.

The coach must ensure the somersault rotation is completed and the rotation is controlled into the landing. A second coach may assist by spotting the landing.

It is reasonable that after setting the snap up correctly with an extended body the gymnast may be permitted to tuck in the somersault phase to ensure sufficient somersault rotation is achieved.

Progression five: Once the above progression can be performed correctly and consist-

Supporting the Tsukahara vault.

ently the vault may now be progressed on to landing on a safety mat placed upon the competition landing area. The coach should initially spot the landing until the gymnast is confident with his or her performance and the coach should then shadow the landing until it is achieved consistently.

Key Points for Coaching the Tsukahara Vault

- A strong but controlled run-up is required to produce forward momentum
- Face the table at take-off to enable forward rotation to be created
- Reach quickly towards the table with the hands
- Ensure the full half turn in the round off is completed before handstand
- A powerful snap up action must be created from the hands
- Once the hands lose contact with the table the arms must drive downward toward the thighs
- A stretched to slightly dished shape should be held throughout the somersault
- The head must remain neutral throughout the somersault but should move forward to sight the floor for landing

- Use the lift of the arms to reduce rotation in preparation for landing
- The feet should land behind the c of m to enable a successful landing to be achieved.

Coaching the Kasamatsu Vault

The description of the Kasamatsu vault differs from that of the Tsukahara vault in that at the point where the gymnast has completed the quarter turn on to the vaulting table he or she makes a further quarter turn in an outwards direction. This results in the gymnast having his or her back to the table rather than the front. This is then followed by the performance of a one and one half front somersault with an added half twist being executed from the hands.

The prerequisites: A powerful run-up, ability to perform a round off with correct technique over the table and good awareness and technique in performing a stretched front somersault with half twist on the floor or rebound situation.

The Tsukaraha vault.

The part Kasamatsu to front landing.

Coaching Progressions for the Kasamatsu Vault

Progression one: Rehearse the round off over the vaulting table to land on to a platform of safety mats at table height.

Progression two: In the same apparatus set up as above, practise the quarter turn on to the table followed by a quarter turn outwards to land on the safety mats with the back to the table.

Progression three: After the thrust from the hands the gymnast should lift the arms and turn the shoulders while driving the heels downward and backward into a three-quarter stretch front somersault. The gymnast must retain good mid-body tension in a dished shape and reach downwards with the hands in readiness for the front body landing. The gymnast should turn the head sideways just before landing in the prone position, and the arms should be bent with control to absorb the impact.

The initial attempts should be supported by the coach from a stable platform placed to the side of the vaulting table and landing area. The coach should place the nearest hand on the front of the torso with the second hand being placed on the lower back. The coach can lift and control the flight and degree of rotation and should remain in contact with the gymnast until a safe landing is executed.

Progression four: Once the orientation skill described above can be performed consistently with height and correct alignment the Kasamatsu vault may be performed over the table into a foam-filled landing pit. The coach may support the gymnast from a stable platform to ensure good technique is attained. As consistency is gained and confidence is gathered the landing should be adjusted progressively to include safety mats placed on top of the foam until the vault can be performed safely and consistently with the safety mats level with the floor.

Progression five: The vault may now progress to the situation illustrated and the coach should assist at the point of the thrust from the hands to ensure the correct flight and rotation are achieved consistently. The initial attempts should be made into a foam-filled landing pit and then progressed on to a safety mat in the landing pit. As the vault progresses to the situation illustrated a trained spotter should be used to spot the landing.

Progression six: A half turn out of the front somersault may now be added to complete the Kasamatsu vault. This should be learned with the landing occurring into a landing pit then progressed on to safety mats placed in the pit. When this progression is performed consistently it may be performed as shown, firstly on to a safety mat and then on to the competition landing module. The coach should continue to provide support, particularly by spotting the landing.

Key Points for Coaching the Kasamatsu Vault

- Ensure the gymnast faces forward at the point of take-off after a strong run-up
- Reach the hands quickly towards the table so that maximum forward momentum is retained on to the table
- Bend the first arm so as not to cause a block against the first hand and to allow a smooth transition into a two-arm thrust
- Quickly lift and turn the arms to ensure the half turn is completed successfully
- Drive the heels downward and backward as the arms move forward and downward into the forward somersault phase
- Drive one arm forward and downward, to initiate the twist then wrap the second hand into the chest to accelerate the twist
- Retain a slightly dished shape throughout the flight
- Lift the arms up and to the side to control the twists and somersault motion in preparation for the landing
- The feet should land in behind the c of m to facilitate a controlled landing.

Kasamatsu with half turn.

The complete Kasamatsu vault.

Adding Twists to the Vault – General Comment:

Each of the core vaults described above will form the basis for more advanced vaults, with higher difficulty tariffs. This will entail adding twists or multiple rotations into the post flight from the table. The techniques used to produce a twist are explained in the chapter on the principles of twisting earlier in this publication.

CHAPTER 15

COACHING ASYMMETRIC BARS/UNEVEN BARS

Commonality Between Men's and Women's Bar Work

Coaches of male or female gymnasts should be aware that many of the skills in each of the disciplines are common and can be taught in a similar way. Please refer to the section on the horizontal bar for further bar skills that are common to both men's and women's artistic gymnastics.

Beth Tweddle on the asymmetric bars.

Training Aids Used on the Bars

Training gymnastic skills on the bars is very punishing on the hands due to the friction with the bar. Blisters are common, painful and can result in considerable time being lost from training. The gymnasts wear leather hand grips, fitted frequently with dowel pegs to protect their hands.

The dowel enhances the grip on the bar but is extremely important to ensure the hand grips are fitted correctly and they do not stretch to the extent the grip may wrap around the bar. This may cause serious injury to the wrists. The coach is advised to inspect the condition of the hand grips frequently since, in addition to stretching, they may snap if they wear too thin. Magnesium carbonate is used on the hands to retain the grasp on the bar.

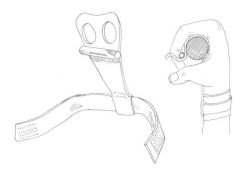

Typical hand grip with dowel.

It takes many hours of training to develop the hard skin necessary to withstand the demands of training and competition and care needs to be taken to ensure the condition of the hands does not deteriorate. The complicated nature of gymnastic skills requires many repetitions to learn and consolidate them. In an effort to protect the hands, training aids such as gloves and loops, or leather or plastic sleeves and loops, are used in conjunction with a polished bar. The sleeves and loops rotate around the bar and reduce the friction on the hands. The loops hold the gymnast on to the bar.

Loops and sleeves.

It is imperative the loops are fitted to suit each individual gymnast and the condition of the equipment is checked frequently. The bar itself must be kept highly polished to ensure the friction between the bar and sleeves is minimal. These very useful training aids may be used when learning many skills that do not require the release and regrasp of the bar.

The Asymmetric Bars

In women's artistic gymnastics the asymmetric, or uneven, bars comprise two fibreglass bars that are parallel but at different heights from the floor. The higher bar is 2.5m and the lower is 1.7m. The bars are 2.4m in length and the distance between the bars is adjustable from 1.3 to 1.8m to accommodate the difference in size of the gymnasts. A 20cm thick landing mat covers the landing area beneath and around the bars.

The regulations for asymmetric bars requires that the gymnast performs elements of giant swing and swings close to the bars, elements that travel from one bar to another, elements with twist and flighted release, and recatch elements. The gymnast must also dismount from the apparatus with a recognized dismount element that is commensurate with the level of difficulty of the main body of the routine.

Like all gymnastic disciplines, there are many skills performed on the asymmetric bars and a small selection of the core skills are described below.

Coaching the Clear Backward Hip Circle

This element can be performed on the high and low bar and is also used within men's artistic gymnastics.

The prerequisites: Good mid-body core strength to be able to hold a strong dished shape, the ability to perform a pencil handstand shape and a backward hip circle. The skill also requires the gymnast to be able to open the arm and shoulder angle powerfully and quickly without loss of body shape.

Coaching Progressions for the Back Hip Circle to Handstand

Progression one: Rehearse the backward hip circle on the low bar ensuring the gymnast can retain a dished shape throughout the skill.

Progression two: Rehearse the backward roll to prone position on the floor with straight

The clear back hip circle.

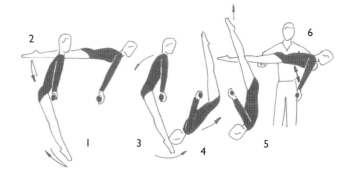

arms ensuring the opening of the shoulder angle is powerful and can be performed without loss of mid-body tension.

Progression three:
The backward hip circle is performed with support from the coach into a front planche finishing position.

The coach should stand on a stable platform to the side of the bar, from which the gymnast will cast into the back hip circle. The gymnast must cast to horizontal then produce a dish shape in the body as the shoulders drop backward. As the gymnast passes under the bar, the opening of the shoulder angle must commence and the coach should reach over the bar to grasp the shins of the gymnast with hand furthest away from the bar.

The second hand should grasp the under the shoulder immediately and continue to support the gymnast through the top planche position to rest on the bar or dismount to land.

Progression four: It is advisable for the gymnast to rehearse the backward roll to handstand on the floor with straight arms as the next progression to reinforce the rapid opening of the shoulder angle.

Progression five: The gymnast should now be ready to progress to performing the clear back hip circle to handstand with support from the coach. The entry will be the same as described for progression three above but the shoulders must drop back with greater

speed to increase the momentum and once the gymnast's shoulders pass under the bar the shoulder angle must be opened rapidly.

The coach can assist in the initial attempts by reaching over the bar and grasping both sides of the gymnast's shins and assisting in the upward movement of the legs.

As the gymnast gains in confidence and the understanding of the movement improves the coach should reduce the amount of support gradually until he or she can resort to shadowing the skill. The coach should ensure the gymnast's feet follow an imaginary vertical line above the bar as the shoulder angle is increased.

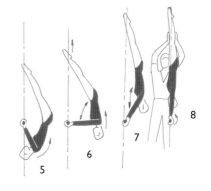

Supporting the back circle to handstand.

Key Points for Coaching the Backward Hip Circle to Handstand

- The gymnast must retain a strong dished body shape throughout the skill
- The head should remain neutral at all times
- The shoulder angle must be opened rapidly
- Remember to rotate the wrists when arriving above the bar to adjust the grip.

Coaching the Stalder Straddle Circle to Handstand

One of the most common close bar skills in women's gymnastics is the Stalder circle. This element was performed initially in men's artistic gymnastics and named after the Swedish gymnast Joseph Stalder, who was the first to perform the skill.

The Technique for the Stalder Circle

Cast from front support into a folded straddle support (Japana position) with the seat vertically above the hands.

The Stalder circle.

The downward swing should commence with the shoulder angle open fully to press the c of m as far as possible from the bar. This produces the maximum angular velocity in the downswing.

The straddled legs should fold quickly into a deep fold and the shoulder angle should be closed to arrive beneath the bar with a full fold of the hips.

As you begin to rise on the upswing the shoulder angle should be opened gradually but the hips must remain in a deep fold to retain the angular momentum for as long as possible.

Once the shoulders have entered the final quarter of the circle the shoulder angle should be opened fully and the legs must then circle sideways into the handstand position. The body should arrive in a dished shape in the handstand.

The prerequisites include: Good flexibility in the hips and the ability to perform the Japana swim round, as described in the section on the straddle lift to handstand; backward roll to handstand with straight arms; and Japana handstand.

Coaching Progressions for the Stalder Circle

Progression one: Rehearse the Japana handstand on a floor bar and circle the legs sideways into the handstand position with the coach supporting at the waist from behind the gymnast.

Progression two: On the floor bar, start in the Japana handstand, with the shoulder angle open fully and while retaining the straddled fold position, fall on to the safety mat.

This will encourage the gymnast to push the c of m away from the bar to generate maximum angular velocity in the downswing.

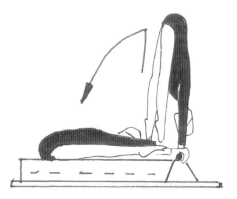

Straddle on a floor bar.

Progression three: On a low bar the gymnast casts into a Japana handstand and then begins the downswing by pushing the c of m as far away from the bar as possible.

During the downswing the straddled legs must be held into the body and as the shoulders pass the horizontal position with the bar, the hips are rotated quickly backward. The gymnast must achieve the complete straddled fold beneath the bar and the legs must press downward into the body.

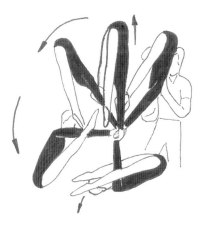

Swing from Japana handstand.

As the upswing starts the fold should be retained to maintain the upward angular momentum.

As the shoulders pass the horizontal, the shoulder angle begins to open but the straddle fold must be held in. At this point the coach may assist the gymnast either under the waist or on the shoulders. The gym-nast should arrive back at the start position in a Japana handstand. This progression can be practised in sets of two or three attempts.

Progression four: The full Stalder circle may now be attempted as described in the section on technique above. The aim is to arrive above the bar in the Japana position and then just before the vertical is reached the legs are circled sideways into the handstand position. The coach can assist in the initial attempts by supporting under the waist or on the shoulders or upper back but care must be taken to avoid inhibiting the straddled legs.

Note: The Stalder circle can be pre-formed in the opposite, forward direction and in this case the skill is called the Endo circle. The technique and progressions are very similar but the Endo is performed in under grasp on the bar and the circle is in a forward direction. The challenge is to keep the straddle fold from unfolding during the upswing. This can be avoided by pushing the feet vertical as the seat starts to rise as this encourages a deeper fold in the body.

Key Points for Coaching the Stalder Circle

- Push the c of m away from the bar on the downswing to maximize the angular momentum
- Hold the straddled legs into the body and rotate the hips rapidly backward into the deep straddled fold position beneath the bar

World Champion Kohei Uchimura during a Stalder circle.

- On the upswing the shoulder angle opens progressively but the straddled fold should be held until just before the vertical position
- With the shoulder angle removed, circle the legs sideways into the handstand position and readjust the hand grip on top of the bar.

Coaching the Backward Giant Swing

The backward giant and forward giant swings are perhaps the most important skills on the bars as these are used to generate the swing momentum into many other skills and for the dismounts. The techniques are similar for men's and women's gymnastics but female gymnasts have to contend with the low bar and therefore adjustments to the technique are required.

The Effect of the Force of Gravity in the Backward Giant Swing
The mechanical principles that will ensure successful completion of the giant swings are:

in the downswing, maximize the angular momentum by extending the body as much as possible. This moves the c of m as far as possible from the pivot point (the bar) to maximize the downward turning effect of the force of gravity that acts through the c of m.

In the upswing, it is necessary to reduce the moment of inertia (m of i) or resistance to rotation in order to reduce the retarding effect of the force of gravity. This is achieved by introducing a dish into the body and closing the shoulder angle slightly during the upswing. This brings the c of m closer to the pivot point and reduces the turning moment created by the force of gravity that tends to decelerate the velocity of the upswing.

The Technique Used in the Backward Giant Swing
Starting in handstand at position (1), the gymnast produces a slight dish into the body and pushes simultaneously downward and forward against the bar. This moves the body into an off balance position and extends the body away from the bar.

This extension is maintained through (2) to (3), at which point the force of gravity has maximum turning effect since the c of m is at its furthest vertical point from the bar.

Once the feet have passed the horizontal (at a point about 120 degrees), a slight dish is introduced by tensioning the front of the body (4). At (5) this tension is then released and the heels are extended backward to create an arch in the body and the gymnast passes under the bar in a fully extended or slightly arched body shape. (6)

The tension in the body created by the arched shape is then used to assist the rapid change of shape as the feet are kicked into a dished shape (7). At the same time, the gymnast begins to press forward against the bar to aid the creation of the dished shape and to close the shoulder angle slightly. The combined effect is to reduce the m of i of the body, which in turn reduces the decelerating effect of the force of gravity.

This body shape is then held through (8) and (9) as the gymnast presses downward on the bar to open the shoulder angle gradually.

Upon reaching the vertical position (10) the gymnast should maintain a slightly dished shape so the feet lead the swing over the bar. The gymnast must adjust his or her grip in the handstand position, relaxing the grip and rotating the hands before reasserting the grip. It is most important the head remains neutral throughout the swing.

The most common errors in the performance of the backward giant swing in the learning stages are:

- Insufficient angular momentum being generated in the downswing to carry the gymnast through the upswing
- When the gymnast presses down on the bar during the upswing, the head may be forced backward, causing the body to arch and resulting in an increase in the m of i and a loss of upward momentum.

The prerequisites: A high level of core strength to be able to control the mid-body and the ability to perform a backward roll to handstand with straight arms while retaining a dished body shape.

It is also very important to introduce some escape drills that can be adopted in an aborted or failed attempt. When insufficient momentum is generated during the upswing the gymnast may:

- Bend the knees to reduce the m of i and retain upward velocity and complete the giant swing
- Rotate the grasp under the bar and retain a dished shape. The coach can then assist by catching the gymnast under the back and legs
- The gymnast may make a half turn by pressing against the bar before dismounting on to his or her feet. The coach may catch the gymnast on the front and rear of the torso.

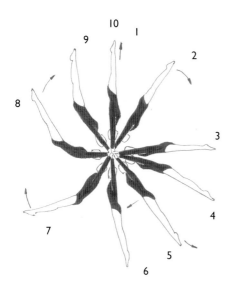

The backward giant.

Coaching Progressions for the Backward Giant Swing

Progression one: Rehearsal of the backward roll to handstand with straight arms.

Progression two: Using a floor level bar and with the hands in over grasp, fall from handstand on to a safety mat with a tensioned and slightly dished body shape. The shoulder angle must be extended fully and the feet should lead the fall on to the safety mat.

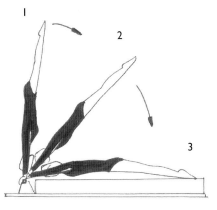

Falling from handstand.

Progression three: Once again using a floor level bar and with the gymnast lying on his or her back on a safety mat, the coach or coaches lift the gymnast into the handstand. The gymnast must retain a dished shape and assist by pressing downwards on the bar. The gymnast must also adjust the grasp on top of the bar.

Progression four: The two progressions described above can then be combined with the lift into handstand preceding the fall on to the safety mat.

Progression five: This progression involves practising the 'tap' or 'timer' action that is a

Rehearsing the upward swing.

key feature of the backward giant. From the hang position beneath the bar the coach should lift the gymnast into a dished shape at position (1). Upon releasing this position the gymnast must arch the body quickly by kicking the heels backward (2). As the vertical position beneath the bar is arrived at the gymnast must press his or her hands forward against the bar and introduce a dish rapidly into the body (3).

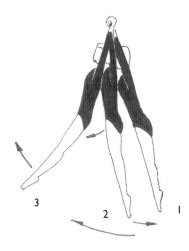

The timer action.

This practice drill provides the gymnast with a good understanding of this important phase of the backward giant.

Progression six: The gymnast should now be ready to learn the backward giant. Start with the gymnast wearing loops and sleeves (or gloves and loops) and working on a polished bar, at waist height to the coach and preferably positioned over a landing pit.

The gymnast casts out in front of the bar and increases the amplitude and momentum of the swing gradually. The timer action is used on each progressively higher swing until sufficient momentum is developed to take the gymnast into handstand. The coach should assist from the side and on the upswing side of the swing by supporting under the legs and shoulders throughout the swing.

The gymnast must be reminded to adjust the grasp in the appropriate direction at the top of each swing.

Progression seven: Once the gymnast is confident in the situation described above a number of giant swings can be combined, with the coach initially supporting as described from the upswing side of the bar but also reaching over the bars to ensure the correct posture in the downswing. Three or four giant swings may be attempted safely in one set. The coach may then reduce the degree of support gradually until 'shadowing' is deemed to be sufficient support.

Progression eight: When the gymnast can perform the skill as described in progression seven with consistency and with correct technique he or she may progress to the normal bar with hand grips and magnesium carbonate.

This progression is best done on a bar over a pit with the bar set at the coach's waist height, but if this is not possible the single bar should be used with the coach assisting from a stable platform at waist height to the bar.

The coach should again stand on the upswing side of the bar, and the support should be provided by the coach stooping to reach under the bar to grasp the wrist of the gymnast with the nearest hand. The gymnast casts into the handstand and swings under the bar, and the coach supports with the second hand under the lower back but retains the grip on the gymnast's wrist. As the gymnast passes over the bar the coach reaches under it to grasp the wrist again before the second downswing occurs.

The greatest point of risk is when the momentum is at its maximum and this is at a point directly under the bar, hence the need for the coach to have a firm grasp of the gymnast's wrist at this point. At this stage of the development the gymnast should have a good understanding of the skill and good spatial awareness in order to make the necessary adjustments to save him or herself in an abortive attempt. If all is well with the performance the gymnast may simply dismount by pushing away from the bar during the downswing. As the gymnast's experience and confidence increases the degree and type of support may be reduced according.

Progression nine: Female gymnasts have to adapt the technique to the A bars and must amend the downswing to accommodate the low bar. This adaptation can be introduced by replacing the lower bar with a rope stretched across the uprights.

During the downswing the gymnast must maintain a stretched position for as long as possible (1 and 2) in order to generate sufficient angular momentum. This is followed by straddling the legs and piking the body sufficiently to just miss the lower bar (3).

Once the legs are past the bar they should join quickly and be forced backward beneath the low bar to maximize the turning moment of the body (4).

The arched shape (5) is followed rapidly by the strong kick into the upswing. When this practice has been mastered a thinly padded lower bar can be introduced.

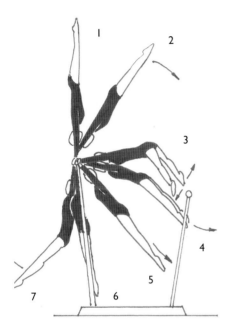

Adapting the back giant to the A bars.

Key Coaching Points for the Backward Giant Swing

- A high level of mid-body control must precede the learning of the giant swing
- Ensure the grasp is secure and in over grasp
- The head must be neutral throughout
- Ensure the gymnast is fully conversant with the safe escape techniques before attempting to teach the BG skill. This will remove a great deal of the anxiety and will bolster confidence
- Ensure the timing action is performed accurately and understood

- Remember the greatest risk occurs immediately under the bar and this is the point where assistance is most needed.

Coaching the Forward Giant Swing

Similar progressions to those used in coaching the backward giant can be adopted when teaching the forward giant skill. The mechanical principles and safety rules are similar and the technique can be understood easily from the illustration below. The main difference is that the forward giant is performed in a forward direction with the grip in under grasp.

Coaching the Double Forward Somersault Dismount

Once the forward giant has been mastered successfully it is relatively easy to develop a front somersault dismount from the swing and then progress this into a double forward somersault dismount (DFSD).

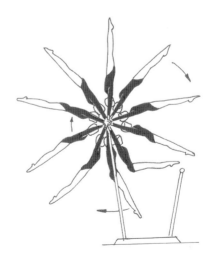

The forward giant swing.

The prerequisites: The ability to perform a powerful forward giant swing and good awareness when performing forward somersaults and double forward somersaults on a trampoline or rebound situation.

The Technique for the Double Front Somersault Dismount

The DFSD is performed from a powerful but conventional forward giant swing in under grasp through phases 1 to 6 but as the vertical line beneath the bar is reached the legs must drive vigorously upward and backward (7).

At this point the shoulders must be passive to allow the legs to rise ahead of the shoulders (8). The hands should push upward against the bar at the release, which must be at the point when the c of m is just below the horizontal line through the bar and with the heels above the shoulders (8).

The moment the hand grip is released on the bar the arms should drive up to grasp the knees as the body is tucked vigorously (9 to 10). A tight tuck is retained in the somersault phase (10 to 11) until the body extends gradually and the arms lift in preparation for the landing (12 to 14).

Coaching Progressions for the DFSD
Progression one: From a cast to handstand, the gymnast swings through the hang beneath the bar and accelerates the heels into the arched release point. With the coach supporting on top of the upper arm and under the thighs, he or she guides the gymnast through a stretched single front somersault to land on a safety mat. Once the correct light and release point has been created the coach releases the grip and re-grasps the gymnast on the front of the upper arm and on rear of the thighs to ensure a safe landing is achieved.

Progression two: The first progression is then performed over a landing pit to ensure the technique is secure. The gymnast precedes the dismount with a forward giant swing and, with the coach supporting to ensure the correct timing of the release point, a stretched forward somersault is performed into the landing pit. The initial attempts should be performed with the arms above the head to limit the speed of rotation to avoid over-rotation.

Progression three: Once the gymnast can control the second progression safely the

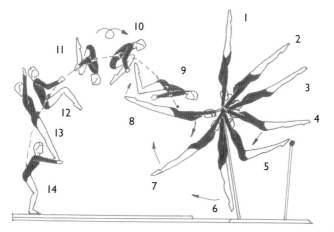

The tucked double front somersault dismount.

double front somersault in the tucked position can be introduced. The gymnast must tuck immediately following the release and drive the arms downwards to grasp the shins. It is recommended that in the initial attempts the preparation for the landing starts slightly early to avoid over-rotation from the double somersault. As the gymnast's awareness improves the correct timing of the landing can be practised.

Progression four: The dismount can then be practised firstly on to one safety mat placed on top of the foam and then the height of the safety mats may be increased gradually to just above floor level as the consistency improves.

Progression five: The full dismount is then performed on to a safety mat placed on top of the normal landing surface. The coach should support at the point of release to ensure correct timing and flight pattern, and then spot the landing to ensure the safety of the gymnast.

Key Coaching Points for the Double Front Somersault Dismount
Ensure that:

- Sufficient angular momentum is generated into the upswing
- The shoulder angle is open fully at the point of release
- The release point occurs just prior to the horizontal line through the bar
- The head remains neutral at the point of release
- Care is taken to make a safe landing

CHAPTER 16

COACHING BALANCE BEAM

Coaching Skills on the Balance Beam

Competition routines on balance beam are required to contain a mixture of tumbles, spins and leaps linked together with choreographed dance-type movements. The competition beam is 5m long, only 10cm wide and stands 1.25m above the floor. Beam work requires a very good sense of balance, a high degree of spatial awareness and great courage to perform the complex skills.

The majority of beam skills are first mastered on floor and then progressed through the following sequence of progressive training situations::

Stage 1: Mastery of the skill on floor.

Stage 2: Performing the skill on a 'beam strip' on the floor to ensure alignment is achieved.

Stage 3: Practising the skill on a floor beam. The floor beam is usually about 20cm high off the floor and may be covered with a protective pad.

Stage 4: Performing the skill on a low beam approximately 80cm high with or without beam-high safety mats to the side or end of the beam. The initial attempts may be performed on a padded beam and progressed to the normal beam surface.

Stage 5: Full height beam with the option of a padded beam and beam-high safety mats placed to the side or end of the beam. As competence, consistency and confidence improves, the pads and safety mats may be removed gradually.

Coaching Beam Sequences

It is extremely important for the gymnast to develop confidence in her ability on the beam and a very good way of enhancing this is to complete a sequence or routine comprising basic drills such as walking forward, backward and sideways on tiptoes; walking with high lifts: spins or turns; intricate and co-ordinated movements of the arms and legs. This requires the gymnast to adjust and maintain her balance automatically while moving along the beam. The more experienced gymnast may include the basic skills such as handstands, backward and forward walk over, cartwheels and simple turns in the sequence.

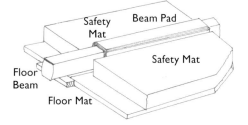

The floor beam station.

Coaching Jumps, Turns and Leaps

The prerequisites: Good general range of movement but specifically a high degree of flexibility in sideways and forward splits; the active range strength to split the legs rapidly while in flight and sound technique in jumping from the solid beam, including consecutive jumps to enable leaps to be linked together.

Typical leaps include the forward or sideways split leap and the ring leap. The ring leap is more difficult since the head is taken backward to touch the raised rear foot, hence sight of the beam is lost making the control of the landing more difficult. A variety of dance-related spins and turns are an integral part of the beam routine and the execution must be accurate in order to maintain the balance and avoid deductions. Spins and turns are usually initiated from a torque turn action against the beam and performed in elevation on the toes.

Ana Pargas performing a ring leap on the beam.

Coaching the Split Leg Backward Somersault

This very dynamic and difficult skill is usually preceded by a round off and a back flip in order to develop the required momentum.

The split leg back somersault.

The Technique for the Split Leg Backward Somersault

On the beam it is necessary for the gymnast to exit the back flip with the feet displaced one behind the other due to the limits of the width of the beam. In this case the lead leg in the split should be the front foot on exit from the back flip. At the take-off the arms should be driven upward and slightly backward while the hips should move upward and slightly forward to initiate the rotation at the point of the take-off. The arms should then be taken sideways to shoulder height as the front leg is lifted vigorously up and towards the chest.

A full split position should be achieved at the highest point in the somersault. The lead leg continues to be forced down towards the beam as the shoulders lift upward and backward. The arms are then raised to slow down the somersault rotation in preparation for landing that should be on the lead leg and immediately followed by the trailing leg. The arms are then opened to the side to assist in maintaining the balance on the beam.

The prerequisites: The gymnast must be able to perform the full combination of round off, back flip and stretched somersault with split legs on the floor successfully and be sufficiently competent and confident at performing a round off back flip on the high beam.

Progressions for Coaching the Split Leg Backward Somersault

The usual sequence of progressive training stations as described earlier should be used and the coach should assist at all stages of development by supporting at the waist from take-off to the landing. The coach should stand on a stable, beam high platform placed to the side of the beam and adjacent to the point of take-off into the somersault. Care should be taken to avoid the gymnast's arms as they are opened wide.

Balances and Artistic Expression

These concepts are two of the many features of beam work that enable the gymnast to apply a personal impression in routines. Balances on the beam range from the standard to the more imaginative using various parts of the body as the base for the balance. Similarly, the spins, the turns and connecting links allow for freedom of expression and are all designed to have the stamp of the individual gymnast on the routine. Examples of the artistic variations are shown in the photographs on this page.

Dismounting from the Beam

It is a requirement that beam routines are completed with a recognized dismount that is commensurate with the level of difficulty of the overall content.

This normally involves the performance of a suitable somersault with or without a twist or twists. Obviously, the dismount would be first mastered on the floor before being developed as a dismount from the beam. Good alignment of the feet on the beam at the point of take-off is essential for safe and successful execution of the complex dismounts.

CHAPTER 17

COACHING MEN'S ARTISTIC GYMNASTIC SKILLS

Men's Artistic Gymnastics

The discipline of men's artistic gymnastics is one of the most demanding of all sports. It requires tremendous levels of strength and fitness and involves very complex skills performed on six pieces of apparatus. The sport is very technical and the demands on the gymnast include incredible levels of spatial awareness and great courage.

The six pieces of apparatus are floor exercise, pommel horse/side horse, still rings, vaulting, parallel bars and horizontal bar. The apparatus are listed in the sequence in which they are normally competed.

Many of the skills described in the section on coaching women's artistic gymnastics are used in men's artistic and the method of coaching the skills is very similar, hence a range of different skills will be covered in this section to avoid duplication. The skills for floor and vault are covered previously in the section on women's artistic gymnastics.

Coaching Skills on the Pommel Horse/Side Horse

The pommel horse, or side horse as it is sometimes known, is one of the most technically demanding apparatus. On this piece of apparatus double leg circles should predominate but the routine must also include shears or scissors movements and may include the very impressive Thomas Flair-type skills. These will be illustrated and described later. The pommel horse is 35cm wide, 160cm long and 115cm high. The top of the pommel handle is 3.4cm in diameter and the distance between the handles can be adjusted between 40 and 45cm.

The competition routines are performed entirely in support on the hands without interruption and this places a great emphasis on upper body strength and endurance.

The physical preparation prerequisites for the pommel horse are a high level of upper body strength in the arms and shoulders, excellent mid-body core strength and good flexibility and active strength in the hips and legs. It is also physically demanding from a strength endurance aspect. Some typical physical preparation exercises related specifically to pommel horse are illustrated and described below.

Physical Preparation for Pommel Horse

Tucked Top Planche
From front support on the pommel horse (PH) the gymnast should press down against the handles to lift the body to the horizontal position. The top planche should be held for a minimum of 3 seconds and the exercise should be repeated in sets of three to five repetitions.

Tucked top planche.

Half lever extensions.

Tucked Russian Lever

From back support the gymnast presses down against the handles to lift the seat upward as high as he can and then holds this position for a minimum of 3 seconds. To be repeated sets of three to five repetitions.

Mid-Body Core Strengthening

The exercise involves holding in sequence the dish, side arch left side, arch and side arch right side body postures. Each position should be held for a minimum of 10 seconds in turn. The sequence should be repeated at least three times.

The tucked Russian Lever.

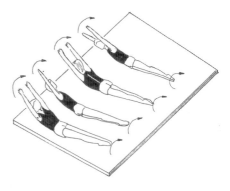

Mid-body strength exercises.

Half Lever Extensions

In the half lever position the gymnast leans the shoulders backward and pushes against the handles to extend the hips forward away from the handles. This exercise should be done in three sets of five.

Strength Endurance for PH

The exercises described above are particularly relevant to learning and performing the double leg circles described below. Strength endurance is particularly important on the PH

Dan Purvis circling with good technique on pommels.

to enable the gymnast to perform routines without the onset of fatigue.

Once the double leg circle has been perfected it is quite normal for the gymnast to try a number of circles without interruption to develop strength endurance. The number of circles performed in one approach to the apparatus will be increased gradually up to around fifty circles. However, care should be taken with young, pre-adolescent gymnasts to avoid the risk of overuse injury to the wrists. The number of circles should be increased progressively over time but if there are symptoms of severe pain developing in the wrists the demand should be reduced.

Double Leg Circle – Direction of Circle

It is firstly important to define the method used to describe the direction of the double leg circle (DLC). When viewed from above, with the gymnast in the back support position, an anticlockwise circle is called a circle

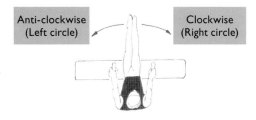

The direction of the circle.

to the left and a clockwise circle is a circle to the right.

The Technique for the Double leg Circle

The illustration shows a clockwise circle to the right. The circle is, in fact, generated from a torque created through the arms, hands and shoulders against the handles. In the clockwise circle the torque is applied against the handles in an anticlockwise direction and due to Newton's Laws of motion this produces an

155

equal and opposite torque that results in the body circling to the right.

However, as a consequence of the body circling in a clockwise direction, there will be a tendency for the body to turn in the same direction and in order to prevent this the body must be rotated intentionally and proportionally in the opposite direction about its longitudinal axis, i.e. in an anticlockwise direction. This enables the gymnast to keep the body in alignment with the hands and shoulders as the body circles around the hands.

The Double Leg Circle to the Right

The aim in the DLC is develop maximum amplitude in the body throughout the circle in order to increase the momentum in the circle. This is achieved by pressing downwards against the horse or handles in order to elevate the hips into an almost straight body position. It is much easier to turn the body around the longitudinal axis if the body is stretched. The circle is actually generated through the hands but in order for the required amplitude to be developed the shoulders must prescribe quite a large circle in advance of the body in order to maintain the balance around the hands. It is also necessary to displace the shoulders continually to allow the hands to be released in turn to allow the body to circle alternately from back support, side support, through front support, passing through the opposite side support and into back support again.

It is essential that the hands re-grasp the handles as quickly as possible so the force through them can be exerted for maximum time to produce the turning moment.

Key Coaching Points for the Double Leg Circle

- Replace the hands as quickly as possible to enable generation of maximum torque

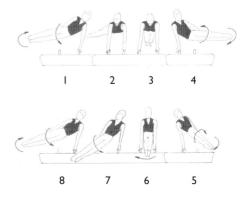

The double leg circle.

- The back support position is the most effective to generate extension and power in the circle
- Maintain amplitude throughout the circle
- In back support – slightly dished shape
- In side support – flank with slight side dished shape
- In front support – slightly arched shape
- Maintain the alignment of the hips with the hands and shoulders.

Progressions for Coaching the DLC

Progression one: Starting in front support position on the floor, walk the feet round to scribe a circle, rotating the body around the long axis so it faces a predetermined fixed point. This will teach the sequence of hand placements and encourage extension in the body.

Progression two: Commencing in a split leg front support position, swing both legs through extended side support to arrive in back support with an extended body. Turn immediately through a half turn around the long axis in the opposite direction to the circle to arrive in front support. Repeat this drill a number of times. This encourages the gymnast to rotate the body continually around the long axis.

Progressions three to nine: Once the basic concept of the DLC has been learned it can then be developed in many different situations, as illustrated below. It is essential that the gymnast can circle on all aspects of the horse to enhance the ability to learn a range of pommel skills.

Progression ten: Once the DLC has been mastered it is essential the strength endurance threshold is raised to enable the gymnast to perform the many repetitions required to learn the skills and to perform the competition routines.

Coaching the Front Shear on Pommel Horse

The regulations require that the gymnast includes some form of single leg swings in their routines and the forward shear (or scissor) is often used to fulfil this requirement.

The variety of training stations.

Forward active leg lifts.

The prerequisites: As with all pommel horse skills, upper body strength is a necessity but so too are flexibility in the hips and strength to lift the legs actively into position. This active range of movement can be developed by lifting the leg into position and then holding the final end position for at least 5 seconds. The exercises should include dynamic leg swings, active leg lifts and held positions to the front, side and rear of the body.

The Technique for the Forward Shear

The illustration shows a forward shear to the right followed by a forward shear to the

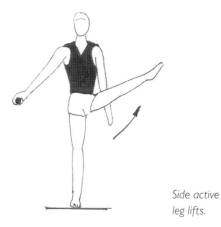

Side active leg lifts.

left. The movement starts from the straddled front support swing. The lead leg is lifted towards the vertical behind the shoulder and the weight is transferred on to the opposite arm. The lower leg rises towards the height of the hips. The hip of the upper leg turns across the horse and as the downswing begins the free arm reaches down to re-grasp the handle behind the leg as quickly as possible. This enables the transference of the weight on to this arm as the upward swing commences.

The leg to the rear of the horse is then swung upward behind the horse and the shoulder to produce maximum amplitude in the upswing. This upward direction of the lead leg is critical to enable the lower leg to be circled across the horse (under cut) before the turn in the upper hip occurs. The hip of the upper leg is then turned across the horse and the downswing commences to complete the shear. The action is then repeated at the opposite side to fulfil the shear requirement.

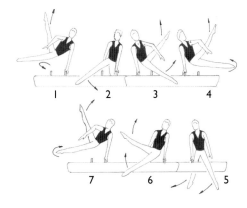

The forward shear.

Coaching Progressions for the Forward Shear

For ease of understanding, the description that follows will relate to a shear to the left.

Progression one: The swing in the straddle position should be developed with good transition of the weight and movement of the shoulders to facilitate good amplitude in the swing. The rear leg (left leg) should remain behind the shoulder line and must not be permitted to cross this line at the top of the swing.

Progression two: Introduce the half shear to the left as follows: from front support, swing the front (right) leg across the horse and drive the rear (left) leg upward behind the shoulder line and transfer the weight on to the right hand. At the top of the swing the front (right) leg under cuts to the rear of the horse while the top leg is held high behind the shoulder line. The half shear to the left can then be repeated in sequence with good amplitude.

Progression three: After completion of the under cut of the lower (right) leg in the half shear the upper (left) hip is rotated forward to enable the right leg to cross the horse to complete the forward shear.

Progression four: The forward shear to the right should then be taught using the same progression.

Progression five: Once both the shear left and the shear right have been mastered they can be combined in sequence but it is important to remember the key points to ensure bad habits do not appear.

Note: It is possible for the coach to assist the gymnast from the rear of the horse by supporting under the top leg but care should be taken not to inhibit the action of the lower leg.

Key Points for Coaching the Forward Shear

- Develop the strength in the active range of movement in the hips
- Introduce the half shear first to avoid the problem of the turn of the upper hip occurring too early, thus prohibiting the elevation of the hips. The half shear may be described as a straddled pendulum swing with the rear leg lifted behind the shoulder while the front leg is under cut beneath the upper leg to finish in straddled front support
- Do not permit the turn of the upper hip to occur before the under cut of the lower leg is complete.

General note: There are many skills on pommel horse but they are mostly a development from the double leg circle and shears as described above. It is essential that the gymnast is able to perform the DLC in all parts of the pommel horse, including facing along the horse, across the horse, on one and both handles and on the body of the horse.

A gymnast with a high level of physical preparation specifically related to pommel horse skills will be able to develop a whole repertoire of skills, including the spectacular Thomas Flairs, travels along the horse in circles and handstand dismounts.

CHAPTER 18

COACHING RINGS

Coaching Still Rings

Competition rules demand that routines contain movements of strength, held positions, swinging elements and a dismount

that is commensurate with the difficulty of the rest of the routine. The top of the ring frame is 5.8m from the floor and the rings are suspended on cables 2.8m above the floor.

The physical prerequisites include: An ability to swing in hang, good mid-body strength and control and a high degree of strength that is specific to the strength elements the gymnast is to learn. The amazing strength elements performed on the rings in modern gymnastics require extraordinary levels of physical power to be developed.

Another feature specific to the rings is that the techniques of the swing are very different to those of the other apparatus. This is due to the fact the point of contact with the apparatus, the rings, actually moves, whereas on the other pieces of apparatus it is fixed. This affects the mechanical principles of the skills on rings as follows:

Held positions: To maintain the balance in held positions, the centre of mass of the body must be directly above or below the centre of the rings, the point of support or suspension.

Swinging: In order to maintain control during the swing, it is necessary for the centre

Kohei Uchimura on the rings.

of mass to travel up and down through an imaginary vertical line below the point of suspension of the ring cables. This is possible since the rings are able to move backward, forward and sideways. This will be clarified in the section below in which the technique for the swing is described.

The Technique for the Swing in Hang on Rings

With the gymnast in inverted hang (1) the movement begins by folding the body into a piked hang (2) and the swing is started with a bent arm pull up and 'cast' (3) into an extended but slightly dished shape. The arms are taken backward as the downswing commences (4). The downswing continues with the upper back leading and with a further slight extension of the body in conjunction with the arms being taken further backward to increase the turning moment in the downswing (5).

The dished shape must be retained as the gymnast passes through the hang phase (6 and 7) but then the heels are driven backward rapidly in the upswing. The body will be arched at this point (8) but the hands and arms must remain passive to enable the body to rotate around the shoulders (9). The hands need to be turned outward to enable the body to tilt around the shoulders. It may be useful to instruct the gymnast to 'force the shoulders downwards' until the feet are driven above the height of the shoulders during this phase of the swing. As the heels approach shoulder height the arms are pushed sideways to enable the legs and hips to rise above the shoulders in order to shorten the path of the c of m during the upswing (10).

Having reached the top of the swing to the rear the chest should lead the downswing and the rings are forced forward to extend the body. This increases the potential to develop momentum in the downswing.

Coaching the Basic Swing in Hang

The coach can assist learning the swing in hang by standing adjacent to the gymnast and supporting as follows during both the **upward and downward swing:**

At the rear: support under the chest and front of the legs

At the front: support under the back of the chest and under the legs.

Coaching the In-location on the Backward Swing

The Technique for the In-Location

The in-location is an extension to the power-

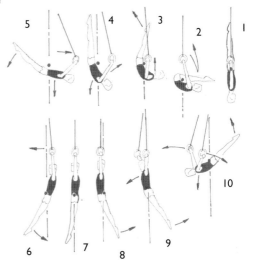

The technique for the swing in hang.

ful rearwards, basic swing (1 to 3 in the illustration below). With the shoulders held down to allow the tilt of the body to occur, the legs continue to drive upward and to the rear (4). From this point the arms press down strongly on the rings to force the c of m in an upward direction. The body shape should change to a slight dish shape to facilitate the press on the rings through the arms and chest (6). The arms will at this point reach at least ring height in the initial learning stages so the arms will be at least horizontal with the rings and the arms will be at their widest point (6). Once the body passes the vertical line through the ring cables the rings begin to move progressively backward and the head should tilt forward towards the chest. This will ensure a smooth transition into the downswing with the upper back and shoulders leading (7).

The gymnast should arrive at the horizontal position with a slight dished shape and with the upper back still leading the swing (8). From this point in the swing, the gymnast is approaching the hang position and the shoulder angle should be open fully at the bottom of the swing (9). Then the gymnast will perform the normal basic swing to the rear.

The prerequisites: a powerful swing in

hang with good technique; a good understanding of the changes in body shape; and the physical strength to press powerfully downward on the rings.

Progressions for Coaching the In-location

Progression one: Rehearse a strong swing in hang with good amplitude to the front and rear of the swing.

Progression two: On a floor mat and springboard, and commencing from a kneeling position facing down the springboard, chest roll down the board placing widespread hands on the floor. Lift the heels over the head while pressing downwards on the hands to lift the body sufficiently to clear the floor with the head. As the body passes the vertical, tilt the head forward towards the chest and roll out forward to lie on the back on the mat.

Progression three: Once the gymnast has sufficient strength on the trolley trainer and can swing powerfully in hang on the rings, the in-location can be attempted with assistance from the coach, as shown in the illustration above.

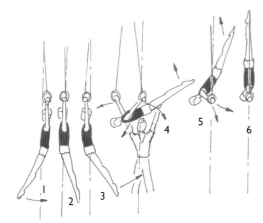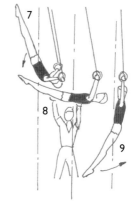

The in-location.

Key Coaching Points

- Develop an efficient swing in hang with correct technique keeping the shoulders passive (down) during the first part of the swing to the rear
- Open the arms wide as the legs drive powerfully upward over the shoulders.
- Close the chest (concave) as the arm press continues
- At the start of the downswing tilt the head forward and maintain the dished shape
- The upper back must lead the down-swing.

Coaching the Dislocation on the Forward Swing

Description of the Technique for the Dislocation

The stretched body dislocation is preceded by a strong downward swinging hang, which is performed in a fully extended body position (1). As the gymnast passes through the vertical hang position the body is arched slightly backward to create a stretch in the muscles on the front of the body (2). This stretch is used to rapidly change the shape of the body into a slight dish and to accelerate the legs into the kick forward and upward (3). As the upward swing begins the shoulders remain passive (i.e. held down) to allow the legs and body to rise quickly above the shoulders. The hands and rings are pressed momentarily forward to assist the leg drive and to close the shoulder angle (4). These actions have the combined effect of reducing the resistance to rotation and simultaneously shortening the path of the c of m in order to maximize the upward momentum. Once the c of m is above the shoulder line the rings should be pulled backward and then open to allow the downward press on the rings to commence (5). This action causes the c of m to rise above the rings and the body should begin to extend above the rings. As the body passes the vertical line the rings are pressed forward progressively and the body should be stretched fully. As the downswing commences the chest should lead the swing to ensure a smooth transition into the downswing.

The prerequisites: A good range of movement in the shoulder extension range and a strong swing in hang with correct technique.

The dislocation.

Progressions for Coaching the Dislocation

Progression one: On a floor mat, with the gymnast in a wide arm handstand, gently fall on to the mat leading with the chest. This action is generally referred to as a 'bale from handstand'.

Progression two: From a standing position on a floor mat the gymnast performs a straight leg, backward roll with straight arms into a wide arm handstand followed by a bale with the chest leading to land face down on the mat.

Progression three: Develop a strong swing in hang and perform a stretched body backward circle, circling above the rings into dismount to land. This progression will allow the gymnast to rehearse the required action during the upswing and the movement of the arms.

Progression four: The full stretched dislocation may now be introduced from a powerful swing. The technique described earlier should be encouraged.

Providing manual support: The coach should support the gymnast at all stages as follows:
- On the downswing: under the chest and under the thighs
- During the upswing: support under the upper back and under the back of the legs.

The degree of support should be reduced gradually as the quality of the performance and confidence improves.

Key Points for Coaching the Dislocation

- Ensure the chest leads and the shoulder angle is open fully during the downswing
- On the upswing the shoulders remain passive as the shoulder angle is closed and the leg drive is introduced
- Ensure the head remains neutral when the downward and forward press on the rings is applied. There is a tendency for the head to be thrown backward as the rings are pulled back on the latter part of the upswing and this should be avoided.

Coaching the Double Back Somersault Dismount

It is a competition requirement on the rings that the routine finishes with a recognized dismount. Perhaps the most common dismount for youth gymnasts is the double back somersault (DBS). If this is learned with correct technique it can be progressed readily into other more difficult dismounts.

The Technique for the Double Back Somersault

The DBS is preceded by a powerful forward swing (1) that is normally generated from a stretched dislocation as described previously in this section. The swing continues as normal through the hang position and initial phases of the upswing (2 to 4).

As the c of m rises above the shoulders and the rings are pulled backward, the legs and hips begin to bend into an open tucked shape (5). The body continues to make an upward circle in this shape and when the c of m rises above the rings they are forced sideways and then released (6). At this point the curved flight path of the c of m has been created and the body shape must be quickly changed to a tight tuck. This is achieved by rapidly forcing the hands forward to grasp the shins (7). This reduces the moment of inertia (m of i) and the velocity of the somersault rotation increases (8). As the body enters the

The double back dismount.

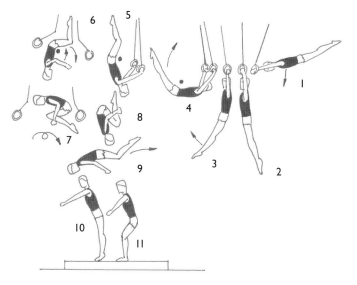

final half rotation the gymnast prepares for the landing by progressively extending at the hips and legs (9).

The arms begin to lift to increase the m of i and the rotation slows down (10). Upon contacting the landing mat the momentum is absorbed by controlled contraction at the hips, knees and ankles (11).

The prerequisites: The ability to perform a double back somersault in the tucked position with correct technique and controlled landing on a trampoline or other rebound situation; the ability to perform a strong swing from a dislocation or similar element into a high stretched backward somersault dismount from the rings.

Progressions for Coaching the Double Back Somersault Dismount
Progression one: From a bale from handstand or high dislocation perform a fast rotating circle up with an open body through to support above the rings. This will avoid an early release from the rings and will instill a good understanding of the path of the c of m.

Progression two: The progression described above is performed into the fast upward circle but as the c of m passes above the rings they are pressed to the side and released. The gymnast should continue to rotate in the stretched position to land on the back on to a safety mat placed on top of a foam-filled landing pit. The body should land in a dished shape with the arms raised above the head to reduce the degree of rotation on landing. This progression will indicate the gymnast can generate sufficient rotation with the correct release point and flight path.

Progression three: The double back in the tucked position may then be attempted into a foam-filled landing pit. The tendency for early release should be resisted and the gymnast should attempt to roll out backward on the landing in the initial attempts. This will reduce the risk of compression injuries to the ankles.

Progression four: As confidence and technique improve the DBS tucked can be progressed as follows to develop spatial awareness and ensure safe landings:

165

- To land on progressively higher safety mats placed on top of the foam in the pits until the mats are at the same level as a safety mat placed on the floor landing area
- To perform the DBS outside the landing pit on to a safety mat. At this stage it is recommended that the coach supports the gymnast at the point of release and upon landing. Support should be provided under the chest and upper back to ensure a safe landing. The support may be reduced gradually to 'shadowing' and then to 'spotting' the landing.

Key Points for Coaching the DBS Dismount

- Ensure sufficient momentum is developed to allow the c of m to rise above ring height
- Ensure the c of m rises above the rings before the rings are released
- The head should remain neutral
- Encourage slight over-rotation upon landings in the learning stages to protect the ankles
- The coach should be vigilant and ready to support the landing.

Coaching Strength Held Elements on Rings

One of the main features of ring routines are the amazing feats of strength that the gymnast performs. These include the cross or inverted cross, which are performed as held parts but the positions are arrived at by either lowering into, pressing out of or swinging into them.

The development of the strength required to perform these amazing feats of strength is a long process. The strength training regime usually involves the gymnast performing a number of repetitions of the held part in various combinations of:

- Lowering into the position (eccentric exercise)
- Holding the final position of the held part (isometric exercise)
- Pressing out of the position (concentric exercise)

The exercises may be performed using elastic strands or weight belts to provide the resistance and the coach may also provide assistance as required.

CHAPTER 19

THE PARALLEL BARS

The routines performed on parallel bars must include predominantly swinging moves in support above the bars and in hang beneath them. Skills may be performed on both bars or on a single bar and may also be performed across them.

The bars are oval shaped, 3.5m long and the bars are 2m from the floor. The width of the bars is adjustable between 42 and 52cm.

The prerequisites: Excellent mid-body core strength; good range of movement in the shoulders; and very good endurance strength in the arms and shoulders.

Coaching the Swing in Support

Perhaps the most important skill on the bars is the swing in support and this essential basic skill is illustrated below.

The Technique for the Swing in Support
The swing starts in the handstand and the c of m must be be pressed as far as possible away from the bar to maximize the potential for the swing (1). The downward swing is initiated by moving the feet forward to create an off balance in the handstand (2). The shoulders move forward slightly to retain control of the swing and as the c of m passes the horizontal, the body shape changes from a dish into an arch as the hips are forced downwards to lead the swing (3). As the gymnast passes through the vertical the body remains arched but the

shoulders are directly above the hands and must be relaxed to remove any restriction to the swing (4).

The legs are then driven forward into a dished shape as the upswing commences and the shoulders begin to tilt backward slightly (5). This is necessary to bring the c of m closer to the pivot point to reduce the retarding effect of gravity and to shorten the upward path of the c of m. As the hips rise above the line through the shoulders the hands press backward against the bars to move the shoulders forward until they are directly above the hands and the body is then extended fully (6).

This is the point at which many of the parallel bar skills are initiated. The body should

Supporting the swing on P bars.

remain extended as the front downswing commences to create maximum momentum (7) and as the body passes the vertical the shoulders must be directly above the hands and again there should be no restrictions in the shoulders.

The heels then are driven backward and the shoulders begin to pivot forward about the hands (8). The shoulders are moved forward to reduce the path of the c of m to retain the upward momentum (9).

As the hips pass above the line through the shoulders the hands are pressed forward against the bars to cause the shoulder angle to open gradually and to control the rotation and momentum (10). The swing should finish in a controlled and fully extended handstand (11).

When teaching the swing the coach should support the gymnast from a stable platform to the side and above the bars as follows:

- On the backward downswing: on the front of the shoulder and under the front of the legs
- On the upswing and forward downswing: on the rear of the shoulder and under the back of the legs
- On the backward upswing: on the front of the shoulder and under the front of the legs.

Coaching the Healey Turn

The Healey turn may be described as a full turn about one arm performed during a backward swing down from handstand. This skill can be performed from a static handstand, from swing or in combination with other skills.

When performed from a held handstand the first action is to force the c of m as high as possible (1) and the turn is created at the point furthest from the contact with the bars.

Hence, as the gymnast pushes the c of m away from the bar the feet are turned in the required direction to produce an equal and opposite turning action (torque) through the hands against the bar (2). The turn of the feet moves the body slightly off balance and this transfers the c of m on to the support arm to start the downswing. One hand is released from the bar to permit this action to occur (3).

This hand is lifted quickly close to the side of the body to reduce the resistance to spin around the long axis of the body (4 and 5). The body should retain a dished shape as it descends from the handstand and the shoulders should be displaced slightly backward as the body falls (6). As the gymnast approaches the horizontal the free hand must reach down quickly towards the bar and should re-grasp the bar before the body passes the horizontal line through the shoulders (8). The gymnast

The Healey turn.

Supporting the Healey turn.

should anticipate the momentum in the swing and be alert to the need to press through the hands and displace the position of the shoulders to accommodate this (9).

The prerequisites: A complete understanding of the swing in support and the principles of creating a twist from the handstand position, and a good range of movement in the shoulder girth.

Progressions for Teaching the Healey Turn

Progression one: Beginning in a handstand on a floor mat on the floor, the Healey turn is performed to land in back support on a safety mat. The coach should provide assistance by standing to the side and grasping hold of the back of the thighs to initiate the turn and move the c of m over the support arm. As the gymnast releases the free arm the coach should release the grasp and replace the hands under the upper back and under the legs to allow the free hand to arrive on the floor mat before the feet meet the safety mat. This supporting technique should be used on each of the progressions described below.

Progression two: The Healey turn is then progressed to a set of floor level parallette

bars, as shown in the illustration. The free hand should attempt to re-grasp the bar before the feet contact the safety mat.

Progression three: Once progression two has been mastered consistently the movement can then be progressed to a situation on the parallel bars with a safety mat placed on top of the bars on the landing side.

Progression four: With the gymnast able to re-grasp the bars consistently the Healey turn can then be perform on padded parallel bars with the coach supporting beneath the bars to support on the upper back and at the legs after the skill has been completed.

Progression five: When the previous progression can be performed correctly and consistently the Healey turn may be performed without the need for pads on the bars but the coach must support beneath the bars in case a mishap occurs.

A further development of this skill is to perform it on the parallel bars from a swing.

Prior to this it is recommended the technique is amended slightly as the turn can be initiated just prior to the handstand position.

The Healey turn on the floor bars.

This can be rehearsed on the floor bar set-up and the turn is preceded by a kick to handstand, as shown in the illustration below.

Coaching the Backward Giant on Parallel Bars

The ability to swing in hang is an important aspect of parallel bars skills and the giant swing is a popular skill in modern day gymnastics routines.

Description of the Backward Giant Swing

Starting in the handstand, the feet are moved into a dished shape to move the body off balance to start the downswing (1). A slight angle is introduced in the shoulders angle to ensure the downswing can be controlled and the body shape should remain dished throughout the downswing (2) until the horizontal position is reached (3). As the body passes the bars the legs begin to bend at the knees (4) to allow the feet to clear the floor as the gymnast enters the hang position below the bars. The gymnast should pass under the bars with the hips leading and the shoulder angle extended fully (5).

As the forward upswing commences the gymnast must press forward through the hands against the bars to close the shoulder angle and to facilitate the upward drive of the knees (6). This reduces the m of i of the body and minimizes the retarding effect of the force of gravity on the body in order to retain the upward momentum of the swing.

Once the c of m has risen above the bars and the body enters the final quarter of the circle the hands are then pressed backward and downward against the bars to begin to open the shoulder angle (7). It should be noted that the bend at the knees and hip angle should remain closed to maintain the upswing until, just prior to the handstand,

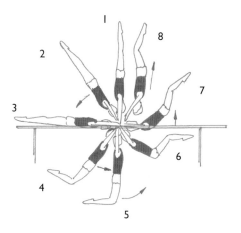

The backward giant swing on parallel bars.

the legs are extended upward. The hand grasp at this point will be in under grasp and the gymnast must release the grip as the momentum lifts the body above the bars (8) and then re-grasp the bars rapidly in over grasp in the handstand position. As the hands re-grasp the bars the gymnast must push downwards against the bars to control the swing (1).

The prerequisites: Mid-body core strength and ability to close and open the shoulder angle rapidly; stability in the handstand; a backward roll to handstand on floor with straight arms and the ability to perform a powerful swing in hang with correct technique.

Progression for Teaching the Backward Giant Swing

Progression one: Rehearsal of a backward roll to handstand with straight arms on the floor.

Progression two: The gymnast should lay on the back at the end of a set of floor parallel bars with the legs bent. The arms are stretched above the head and in between the bars with the hands resting on the bars in a cupped shape with the fingers pointing outwards. Two coaches then lift the gymnast towards the handstand so the gymnast experiences the unusual hand grip on the bars. The grip must be retained until the bent leg handstand position is achieved in an inverted grip. The purpose of this drill is to avoid an early kick of the legs, which will result in an early release of the grip on the bars.

Progression three: In the same set up as in progression two, as the gymnast approaches the handstand the legs kick out straight and the hands release and re-grasp the bars into the handstand.

Progression four: The next stage is to practise the swing from support into the hang position. From a swing in support facing inwards on the end of the bars, the gymnast swings until the legs reach around shoulder height on the backswing. The gymnast should then cast into the downswing with a slightly dished shape and with a slight angle in the shoulders. The coach should support the gymnast under the chest and under the thighs in order to control the swing and regulate the correct technique and shape in the swing.

Progression five: The bale from handstand may then be introduced with the gymnast beginning in handstand, facing inwards on the end of the bars and swinging down into a safety mat, as shown in the illustration. The bale should mirror the technique of that to be used in the giant swing and the coach should support the gymnast under the chest and thighs to decelerate him or her towards the bottom of the swing and into the safety mat.

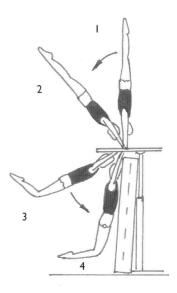

The swing into hang.

Progression six: Once each of the previous progressions has been mastered, the first attempts can be made at the giant swing.

This practice should be performed on the end of the bars facing outwards. This provides the coach with the best position to give maximum support to the gymnast.

This is particularly important at the point when the gymnast passes through the hang position into the upswing as this is when the gymnast is at greatest risk.

From the handstand the gymnast bales into the downswing (I) and into the hang phase (2 and 3).

The coach (or coaches), standing on stable platforms, adjacent to the gymnast should reach between the bars with the nearest arm and grasp the gymnast's upper arm with a rotated grip (fingers pointing towards the gymnast's arm).

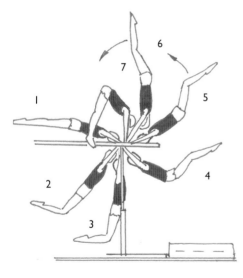

Supporting the giant swing.

This contact should be made just before the full hang position (3). As the gymnast swings upward the coach should grasp behind

the thighs with the second hand at point (4) and then assist the gymnast to continue the swing (5) towards the handstand.

In the initial attempts it is advised that the gymnast retains the grasp and finishes the swing by pressing through the hands and straddling the legs from the handstand to stand on the bars. This will boost the gymnast's confidence by introducing a safe outlet at the end of the skill. It is also advisable to teach the gymnast to handspring to land from the end of the bars with the coach still retaining the grip on the arms and legs as this will give another useful escape route in the event of an aborted attempt.

Progression seven: Once the gymnast can perform the above progression with confidence and correct technique the complete giant swing may then be attempted in the centre of the bars. At this stage the coach should provide support beneath the bars as follows:

- On the downswing: under the chest and under the front of the thighs
- On the upswing: under the back and on the back of the thighs.

As the level of competence and confidence increases the degree of support can be reduced accordingly.

Note: You may have noticed the gymnasts carefully preparing the parallel bars at an event by chalking the bars and putting a sticky liquid either on the bars or on their hands. This is to ensure they have sufficient grip when performing the various under bar swings.

Key Coaching Points for the Backward Giant Swing

- Ensure the bars are prepared suitably to provide the appropriate grip

- Do not permit the head to be forced backward during the upswing as this will tend to cause the chest to lift, resulting in the shoulder angle opening prematurely and the leg extension occurring too soon
- Remember to teach the safe outlets for use in the event of a failed or aborted attempt as this will remove some of the anxiety from the gymnast.

Coaching the Piked Double Backward Somersault

The most frequently used dismount from the parallel bars, the piked double backward somersault (PDBS) is a highly rated skill and will normally be commensurate with the difficulty of the remainder of the routine.

Description of the Technique for the PDBS

The PDBS normally commences from the handstand (1) and the initial downswing is performed in an extended or slightly dished shape (2) with the shoulders moving forward slightly to allow the amount of swing to be controlled. Just before the horizontal line through the shoulders is reached the hips are extended into an arched shape to pre-stretch the muscles on the front of the body (3).

As the vertical line is approached the shoulders must be relaxed to avoid restriction and the legs begin the upward and forward drive (4). The shoulders must lean backward to bring the path of the c of m closer to a vertical line through the hands to reduce the retarding effect of the force of gravity during the upswing (5). The powerful upswing continues until the hips reach shoulder height. At this point the gymnast presses the hands backward and sideways against the bars to affect the upward and sideways flight path of the c of m. The hands release the bar with the hips circling above the shoulders (6) and the body shape must change rapidly into the piked shape to reduce the resistance to rotation (m of i). The hands grasp the underside of the knees to hold the tight pike shape throughout the double somersault (7 to 9).

As the c of m passes the height of the bars the body begins to extend in preparation for the landing (10).

The prerequisites: The ability to perform a PDBS with correct technique on the trampoline or rebound situation; and a tucked

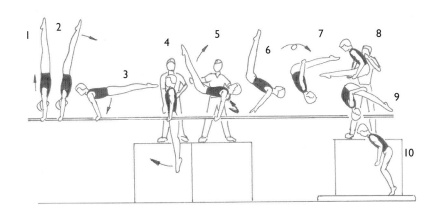

The piked double back dismount.

double back somersault dismount from the P bars with good height and rotation.

Progressions for Coaching the PDBS

The sequence of progressions are similar for both the double backward somersault performed in the tucked or piked body shape, hence we assume the gymnast has success-fully mastered the tucked double back somersault dismount.

Progression one: The gymnast rehearses the swing and release into an open piked single somersault to land on the back on to a pile of safety mats at just above the height of the bars. This will ensure the gymnast is able to create the correct technique with sufficient height in the flight.

Progression two: This requires a train-ing situation where the parallel bars are adjacent to a foam landing pit and with the coach assisting from a suitable stable plat-form to the side of the bars. The gymnast first practises a high tucked back double somersault with sufficient rotation to allow a 'kick out' to land in the pit. The PDBS may then be attempted, with assistance from the coach supporting at the centre of the upper back to control and ensure the correct shoulder movement, and under the thighs to ensure sufficient lift and rotation. The gymnast should be encouraged to retain the piked shape to slightly over-rotate on landing.

Progression three: As the performance and confidence improves the PDBS can be performed in the same situation as in progres-sion two but with safety mats being placed on the foam inside the landing pit. The height of the mats can be increased gradually until the mats are at a height equivalent to the height of a safety mat placed on the normal landing surface.

Progression four: Once the gymnast can demonstrate consistent, safe and correct technique in the situation described above the training station can progress to the normal competition set-up but with a safety mat placed on the landing surface. The coach should assist the gymnast as described above and the gymnast should again be encouraged to slightly over-rotate the land-ing to avoid injuries to the ankles. The degree of support can be reduced as consistency is achieved.

Progression five: When the gymnast has gained in confidence and is able to perform the PDBS consistently on to the safety mat without assistance the coach should stand behind and to the side of the point of landing to spot the landing.

Progression six: The skill should then be transferred on to the competition land-ing surface and again the gymnast should be encouraged to slightly over-rotate the initial attempts until the spatial awareness is good. The dismount should then be practised after the penultimate skill and then with the other preceding skills being progressively added before the dismount.

Key Points for Coaching the DBS Dismount

- Generate a powerful downswing and relax in the shoulders
- The shoulders must lean slightly backward on the upswing
- The hips must swing to a point above the shoulder line
- Press the bar downward, backward and sideways to direct the flight path
- Keep the head neutral.

CHAPTER 20

THE HORIZONTAL BAR

Please note: Many of the skills for horizontal bar are similar to those used on uneven bars and may be developed with similar techniques and coaching progressions, so please refer to the section on uneven bars.

Competitive routines on the horizontal bar (HB) must be composed entirely of swinging elements with no stops permitted. The skills must include elements in the extended shape, i.e. forward and backward giant swings in various hand grips with and without turns, and elements that are performed close to the bar. The bar is 2.8cm in diameter, 240cm long and 280cm from the floor.

The general prerequisites: A very good range of movement in the shoulders and hips; excellent mid-body core strength; and a high level of spatial and body awareness and great courage. The various HB skills will have physical requirements specific to that skill and these will be identified within the individual descriptions.

Coaching the Endo Circle with Half Turn

The Endo circle is classified as a close bar skill and it may be described as a free, straddled circle forward from handstand to handstand performed in under grasp. The Endo is closely related to and almost the exact opposite of the Stalder circle, previously described in the section on uneven bars. The Stalder circle is performed in a backward direction in over grasp.

The Technique Used in the Endo Circle with Half Turn to Handstand

With the hands in under grasp the gymnast moves off balance in handstand to start the downswing (1). While pressing against the bar to keep the shoulder angle open the gymnast straddles the legs and begins to fold the body at the hips (2). The deep fold of the body must

Kristian Thomas on the horizontal bar.

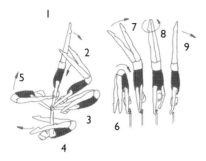

The Endo circle with half turn to handstand.

be completed before the hips drop below bar height (3) and the legs are forced into an inverted figure four shape directly beneath the bars (4). As the upswing commences the seat will tend to drop. This must be resisted by pressing downwards against the bar as the legs are sucked into the chest (5). This deep fold is maintained until just before the Japana handstand is achieved with the shoulder angle fully open (6). The gymnast must press downward against the bar and unfold the straddle, and then start the turning action quickly from the closing feet (7). One hand will be released (8) and the feet will come together to speed up the half turn into the handstand, at which point the free hand re-grasps the bar in over grasp (9).

The prerequisites: Flexibility in the hips and the ability to perform a straddle lift to handstand with correct and efficient technique.

Coaching Progressions for the Endo Circle Half Turn

Progression one: Starting in a straddled half lever in under grasp on a floor bar, with the coach assisting at the hips, lift to Japana handstand and circle the legs sideways towards handstand. As the feet approach the handstand introduce the half turn by turning the feet and pressing down on the bar and simultaneously shifting the weight on to one arm. Release the unweighted hand, complete the turn while closing the feet together and re-grasp the bar in over grasp in handstand.

Progression two: On a low bar station, rehearse the Endo circle from Japana handstand, then progress to finishing the Endo circle in handstand.

Progression three: Once progression two can be performed consistently with efficiency and good technique the half turn may be added as the gymnast approaches the handstand.

Key Coaching Points for the Endo Circle Half Turn

- When creating the straddle into the fold keep the c of m as far away from the bar as possible to create maximum momentum in the downswing
- During the straddled circle keep the legs pressed firmly into the chest to maintain the deep body fold
- Retain the fold in the body on the upswing until the c of m is above the bar, then open the shoulder angle
- Just before the vertical, circle the legs sideways into the handstand and start the turn with the feet
- Transfer the weight on to one arm, complete the turn and re-grasp the bar in handstand.

Coaching the Stoop in Half Turn to Handstand

Another fairly common close bar skill is the stoop in half turn to handstand as illustrated below.

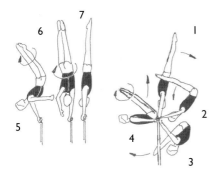

The stoop in half turn to handstand.

The Technique for the Stoop in Half Turn to Handstand

From the exit from the forward giant swing the body passes the vertical (1) and then begins immediately to fold quickly into a piked shape (the stoop) while keeping the shoulder angle open (2). The feet must pass the arms before the seat passes the horizontal line through the bar and then the deep fold should be completed before the shoulders pass under the bar (3). At the start of the upswing the gymnast presses down on the bar to cause the seat to rise, but the fold in the body is retained (4).

As the shoulders reach bar height the body begins to extend as the press downward against the bar continues. This has the effect of converting the circular motion of the swing to a more vertical motion, raising the c of m in an upward direction (5). At this point the turn is initiated by turning the feet while continuing to press on the bar. The result is an equal and opposite reaction against the bar and the gymnast must press against the bar to transfer the weight and c of m on to the support arm. The legs must be directed into the turn as the free arm is released and driven upward rapidly and across the chest. The turn

continues around the support arm as the body continues to rise and to extend (6). The free hand should then re-grasp the bar quickly in over grip to complete the skill (7).

The prerequisites: Excellent flexibility in the lower back and hamstrings to enable a full fold of the body to be achieved and good shoulder mobility.

Coaching Progressions for the Stoop in Half Turn to Handstand

Progression one: With the gymnast lying on the back on a floor mat and holding a pole above the head, the legs are raised upward and then stooped in between the arms before the shoulder angle is closed to create the stoop action.

Progression two: From a back support position on the bar, the seat is lifted to raise the c of m before stooping forward and completing a stoop circle forward.

Progression three: In a low bar station, the gymnast casts to handstand in under grasp and then stoops into a forward stoop circle to back support on the bar.

Progression four: Once progression three can be performed with sufficient momentum in the upswing the half turn may be attempted. On the upswing the gymnast presses down against the bar and as the body extends the turn is initiated by turning the legs and feet.

The gymnast should release the unweighted hand to make the half turn and re-grasp as the body passes over the bar to stand on the floor mats.

In the initial attempts the body should be directed intentionally over the bar until orientation and technique improve. The coach should support from a stable platform and on the upswing side of the bar to ensure the safety of the gymnast.

Progression five: Once the gymnast has a full understanding of the skill it can be progressed to a full height bar over a landing pit or over a safety mat. The skill is preceded by a forward giant swing in order to increase the momentum for the upswing. The full skill is attempted with the initial attempts made to cross the bar to release and land into the pit. As confidence grows the turn should occur progressively early until it can be completed into the handstand position, at which point the gymnast may swing down in to a giant swing.

Key Points for Coaching the Stoop in Half Turn Out

- The stoop in must occur with the c of m as far from the bar as possible to maximize the generation of momentum
- The deep fold (pike) must be held until the shoulders arrive above the horizontal
- As the body begins to extend the feet must start the turn and the legs must be directed towards the support arm to transfer the weight on to the support arm
- The free arm should be kept close to the body to facilitate the turn, and the hand must re-grasp the bar as quickly as possible to control the exit into handstand.

Coaching the Backward Giant Swing with Half Turn

There are a number of different turns that can be made during the giant swing on the bar (or bars) and the common factor is that the turn is initiated by the feet, these being the point furthest away from the bar. The feet are turned in the direction of the intended turn and the effect is to create an equal and opposite reac-

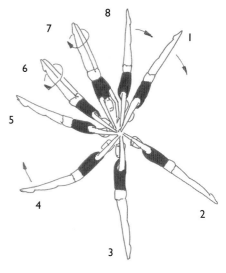

The blind turn.

tion force through the hands against the bar. This reaction force can then be increased by pressing against the bar with the arm that is to become the release arm and this increases the turning moment on the body. This principle can be seen in the illustration of the backward giant half turn or blind turn.

The Technique used in the Blind Turn

This skill is often referred to as the blind turn since the gymnast loses sight of the bar as he or she makes the half turn. The description is for a blind turn around the left arm.

The gymnast performs a conventional backward giant swing until the body passes above the horizontal with the bar on the upswing (1 to 5). At a point approximately 30 degrees prior to the handstand (6) the feet and legs are turned to the left and the right arm presses backward against the bar. The reaction force created by the turn of the feet and the backward force against the bar combine to increase the turning moment about the support arm. The momentum will continue the swing towards the handstand and as the weight is transferred on to the support arm the free hand is released. The half turn of the body around the support arm should occur with the head in a neutral position and the free hand should remain close to the bar during the turn (7).

As the turn is nearing completion the gymnast should regain sight of the bar and then re-grasp the bar in under grasp (8) in order to enter the forward giant swing.

The prerequisites: The ability to perform both the backward and forward giant swing with correct technique, and good mid-body core strength.

Coaching Progressions for the Blind Turn

Progression one: On a floor mat practise a backward roll with half turn into handstand with straight arms.

Progression two: From lying on the back holding a floor bar in overgrasp the coach lifts the gymnast through the half turn into the handstand with re-grasp into mixed grasp. The gymnast must initiate the turn with the feet and with a slightly dished body shape.

Progression three: On the bar at full height and preferably over a landing pit, perform a swing to above the horizontal with the bar and half turn into momentary mixed grasp and quickly re-grasp in over grasp and repeat the drill three to four times.

Progression four: The coach provides support at the hips whilst standing on a stable platform on the upswing side of the bar. The gymnast performs a swing with half turn into handstand into under grasp followed immediately by a half turn to pass over the bar and re-grasp in over grasp. The drill is then repeated.

Progression five: With the coach assisting at the hips, the gymnast performs the complete blind turn into under grasp and continues to swing into a forward giant swing. The skill can then be performed over a normal landing surface with the coach being ever vigilant and ready to support in the event of any erroneous attempts.

Key Points for Coaching the Blind Turn
- Initiate the turn with the legs and feet
- Press backward against the release arm to transfer the weight on to the support arm and to increase the turning moment
- Retain a dished shape until the handstand is achieved
- Head remains neutral throughout the skill.

Coaching the Rybalko Turn

A fairly popular extension of the blind turn is the one and a half turn through the handstand during a backward giant swing, which is normally called the Rybalko turn.

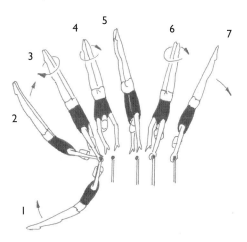

Rybalko turn.

The Technique for the Rybalko Turn

The Rybalko turn is preceded by a backward giant swing (1). Once the body has passed the horizontal with the bar the turn is initiated with the feet and legs turning in the direction of the intended turn in a similar manner to the blind turn (2). Once the turn has started, the hands press downwards on the bar and release it just before the handstand (3). With the gymnast in an upward flight above the bar the body continues to turn around the long axes of the body (4 and 5). The hands should remain close to the bar and the hand leading the turn re-grasps the bar in over grasp and the body continues to turn around this support arm (6) making a further half turn. The free hand then re-grasps the bar in elgrip (rotated and inverted grasp) as quickly and as close to handstand as possible (7) and the gymnast continues to swing down in this new elgrip.

The prerequisites: Consistent performance of the backward and forward giants and the blind turn, and complete understanding of initiating turn with the feet and legs and good spatial awareness around the horizontal bar. The gymnast must also be familiar with swinging in the elgrip grasp.

Progression for Coaching the Rybalko Turn

Each of these progressions should be performed on the horizontal bar erected over a foam-filled landing pit.

Progression one: Rehearse the blind turn from a backward giant and then make an immediate half turn into over-grasp into handstand in the same direction as the initial turn.

Progression two: Repeat the above drill but press downward on the bar and release it after initiating the turn and complete the second half turn during the flight to re-grasp the bar in over grasp. The drill should be repeated until the gymnast is aligned correctly with the bar on the re-grasp.

Progression three: The gymnast should rehearse the swing in elgrip hand and then progress to re-grasping the bar after making the flighted one and a half turn. The gymnast should attempt to re-grasp the bar with the free hand but should then dismount from the bar as the downswing passes the horizontal and before the vertical beneath the bar is reached. This must be repeated until the skill is performed consistently with correct technique and good alignment at the point of re-grasp on the bar.

Progression four: The full Rybalko turn can then be performed with the coach providing assistance to retard the momentum of the swing as the gymnast approaches the hang position beneath the bar. The coach must reach up to make contact with the gymnast as early as possible during the downswing before the full momentum is generated.

Progression five: Only after the skill can be performed safely with consistency and with correct technique can it be transferred to the conventional horizontal bar situation.

Again the coach must provide assistance as described above in the initial attempts and as confidence grows the degree of support may be decreased progressively.

Key Points for Coaching the Rybalko Turn

- The safety of the gymnast must be the prime concern, so ensure each progression is mastered completely and consistently before progressing
- The head must remain neutral throughout the skill
- The turn must be generated from the feet, the legs and hips before the release point

- Ensure the flight direction is cor-rect and that the turn is aligned square to the bar.

Coaching the Double Backward Somersault Dismount

One of the more frequently used horizontal bar core dismounts is the tucked double backward somersault (TDBS), which can be developed into the more advanced variations in the piked or stretched body shape.

The prerequisites: A complete understanding of the backward giant swing, and competence in the performance of a TDBS on the trampoline or rebound situation.

The Technique for the Tucked Double Backward Somersault

The backward giant swing preceding the dismount (1) is adapted just prior to the vertical by closing the shoulder angle and dishing the body (2). This reduces the path of the c of m and allows the speed of the swing to be accelerated across the bar to increase its momentum. This shape is held in the downswing (3) until the timing action is introduced (4), where the shoulder angle is opened and the heels are forced momentarily backward (5). This stretches the muscles on the front of the body to facilitate the kick of the legs on the upswing (6).

As the body contin-

ues to rise, the gymnast must bend gradually at the hips and begin to bend the knees until the release point just below the horizontal is reached (7). At this point the shins should be horizontal and facing directly upward momentarily and the shoulder angle must be open fully. The gymnast should press upward against the bar and then release the grip on it immediately. This press against the bar creates a reaction from the bar to add to the rotation and improves the ability to create the tucked shape.

Once the bar has been released the height and direction of the flight path have been determined. The angular momentum of the body has been fixed. Immediately the hands release the bar the arms should drive upward to enable the hands to grasp the shins and the body is pulled into a tight tucked shape (8). This shape is held through the somersault phase (9) and the majority of the TDBS should be completed before the top of the flight path is reached (10). As the body begins to descend, the gymnast must prepare for the landing by opening out the tuck gradually and lifting the arms (11) to increase the m of i in order to decelerate the somersault rotation

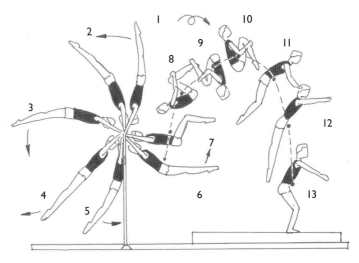

The double back dismount.

(11). The gymnast should now be able to see the landing mat and must absorb the impact of landing by controlled bending of the hips, the knees and ankles and circling the arms if necessary (12).

Progressions for Coaching the TBDS

Progression one: Practise the TDBS on a trampoline or rebound situation.

Progression two: Introduce the modified accelerated backward giant repeatedly without releasing the bar to establish the timing and correct technique.

Progression three: On a full height bar over a foam-filled landing pit, practise the accelerated giant swing in to a one and a quarter stretched somersault to land on the back in the foam. This will indicate that sufficient momentum is being generated and also that the correct release point is understood.

Progression four: The full TBDS may now be performed over the landing pit with the coach shadowing the gymnast at the point of release to ensure the trajectory is correct.

Once this progression is performed consistently safety mats may be placed on top of the foam at increasing heights until a height of mats just above floor level is achieved.

Progression five: Once the gymnast is performing the dismount consistently in the situation described above the TBDS may be performed in the conventional competition situation on to a safety mat. The coach should shadow the gymnast initially at the point of release to ensure the correct release point and trajectory is achieved, while a second coach spots the landing. Once the coach and gymnast are satisfied the release point and trajectory are consistent the coach may then just spot the landing.

Dan Purvis dismounting from the horizontal bar.

Note: When the TBDS is to be introduced into a routine it is recommended the preceding skill is practised initially in combination with the dismount. The penultimate skill can then be added to this combination and then pro-gressively more skills can precede the dismount.

Key Points for Coaching the TBDS Dismount

- Ensure the gymnast has a full understanding of the TBDS in a rebound situation before beginning learning the dismount
- The accelerated giant swing and release point should be performed consistently prior to the TBDS being attempted
- The timing action is critical to producing the correct release and trajectory
- The shoulder angle must be open fully just prior to the release point
- The head must remain neutral throughout the TBDS.

CHAPTER 21

PREPARING FOR COMPETITIONS

The Rules for Competitions

The world governing body for gymnastics, the Fédération Internationale de Gymnastique (FIG) has developed a set of rules for each separate discipline of gymnastics called the code of points. These include the rules of competition, how routines should be constructed and how they will be judged at international and world championships.

The individual national governing body, for instance British Gymnastics (BG) or the United States Gymnastic Federation (USGF), will use these rules for their national senior championships but may choose to adapt them according to the level of competition for younger gymnasts.

Each competitive event will have its own set of rules and regulations derived from the international code of points but designed to meet the specific needs of different categories of gymnasts.

A set of appointed qualified judges will assess each performance according to the appropriate set of rules and judge the routine according to its difficulty, structure and level of performance in order to rank it.

The difficulty of each gymnastic element is given a rating from A, the easiest, with a value of 0.1 points through to G, the most difficult and complex element, which has a rating of 0.7 points.

The elements are also separated into groups according to the type of element. For example, forward somersaults are in one category and backward somersaults are in another. The routine on each apparatus is required to include movements from each of the grouped elements.

One group of judges will add together the nine (for men) or seven (for women) highest value elements and deduct points for each

Koko Tsurumi on the beam.

missing group element to determine the difficulty value or start value for the routine.

A second group of judges then evaluates the execution and presentation (the level of performance) of the routine. The execution judges will deduct points for errors such as bending or separation of the legs, or steps on landing, from a start score of ten points.

The final score is derived by adding the difficulty score to the execution score. This score then determines the ranking of the gymnasts on each individual apparatus and the combined scores on each apparatus determine the individual, all round winner.

In a team event a pre-stated number of individual scores on each apparatus (say three from four) competitors are combined to determine the team total and the highest total is the winner.

This is only an overview of how the routines are structured and judged and it is recommended any person entering into coaching competitive gymnastics should become familiar with the rules and code of points.

Designing Competition Routines

We have learned that each gymnast possesses specific natural abilities and that the individual will have a liking or penchant for particular types of skills. Some gymnasts are powerful and dynamic, while others are more flexible or elegant. The taller and usually slimmer gymnast will often be able to spin or twist more easily around the longitudinal axis of the body, while the more compact and often more dynamic gymnasts will usually be more able to spin or rotate around the horizontal axis of the body.

It is therefore very important to identify the strengths of each gymnast when constructing and long term planning the individual gymnast's routines. In the early years of a gymnast's career it is import to develop a wide range of core or foundation skills upon which the more advanced skills can be based. During this period of development the coach will gain a good understand of which type of skills each gymnast performs well, those they have difficulty with and the gymnast's preferred types. This information can be used to good effect when planning the long term development of competition routines.

It is advisable to start with a core or foundation routine that can be developed over time without having to dismantle it and start again. The advantages of this philosophy are that the gymnast over-learns the basic structure of the routine and develops, over time, the required fitness to perform it. As the gymnast learns progressively more difficult skills they can be substituted in the place of other similar skills without disrupting the structure and understanding of the routine.

The basic structure of the initial routines should try to meet the requirement to include the different categories or groups of elements. The degree of difficulty can then be increased over time as the gymnast masters higher valued difficult elements.

Training for Competition

In the section on planning the training we described how the annual training calendar was subdivided into four phases, namely transition, preparation, pre-competition and competition. The content of these can be briefly described as:

Transition phase: Active rest, general fitness and practise of core elements.

Preparation phase: General and specific physical preparation, learning and perfection of individual skills.

Pre-competition phase: Specific physical preparation, perfection of combinations of elements, part and full competition routines.

Competition phase: Specific physical preparation and consolidation of competition routines.

The duration of each phase of training is broadly the same and dependent on how many cycles of training had been set in the year. Hopefully, with good planning the content of the competition routines and foundation of fitness will have been established during the first two phases of the training and it can now progress to the latter two phases.

The Pre-Competition Phase of Training
During this phase the training should focus on:

* Enhancing the level of specific physical preparation, including three repetitions of simplified core routines to improve endurance strength and cardiovascular fitness
* Perfecting the performance and consistency of the individual skills
* Combining sequences of skills in the order in which they will be performed in the routine
* Repetition of landings from dismounts, including dismounts performed following combinations of preceding skills
* Numerous half routines and a number of repetitions of full routines

This phase of training should ensure the gymnast is prepared appropriately to enter the final phase of the training.

The Competition Phase of Training
The emphasis on the training in this phase is predominately on the consistency of routines, the security of landings from the dismounts and the mental focus on the forthcoming events. The content of the training programme in the Competition Phase should therefore include:

Physical Aspects
* Repetition of mainly full routines (up to 50 of each routine is recommended)
* Accuracy and consistency of dismounts on each routine
* Consolidation of any insecure elements
* The load demands for the sessions should increase gradually to a point about two weeks prior to the main event (peaking) and then be reduced to a lower demand for the last two weeks. This often called tapering and the main focus during this period is on mental focusing.

Mental Aspects
* Mental preparation including: mental imaging, positive self-talk and so on
* Focusing attention and being confident before approaching the apparatus.

General Targets
It is recommended the general scenario for the sessions are varied by:

* Setting the focus on 'clean' routines or no more than two medium level errors in the session
* Varying the load demand for each session from high, medium and low loads to avoid fatigue and enhance recovery between sessions
* Starting on a different apparatus to ensure the same apparatus does not come late in each session
* Setting the number of routines higher on the first apparatus station while the gymnast is fresher and lower later in the session.

'What If' Scenarios

In order to prepare the gymnast for the multitude of things that can interrupt or influence him or her during competitions the inclusion of 'what if' scenarios is recommended:

- Have the gymnast's peers appraise the performance of the gymnast, including level of determination, attitude and so on
- Having a qualified judge score the routine and provide critical feedback
- Introducing distractions such as people talking or playing loud music during performances
- Interrupting the concentration by delaying the readiness of the judges.

This phase of the training can become tedious and intense and it may be a good tactic to intersperse training routines with sessions where the gymnasts are introduced to new elements that are intended for inclusion in future routines.

As a coach you will almost certainly come across the gymnast who suddenly develops the 'self-doubt' syndrome in which he or she loses confidence in his or her ability to perform a routine or particular element. This is most likely to occur during the week preceding an event but can appear at the actual competition. The likelihood of this situation occurring increases as the level of expectation on the gymnast rises. To address this scenario it is recommended that you:

- Let the gymnast know it is not an uncommon situation
- Reinforce your belief and confidence in him or her
- Remind the gymnast of the many times he or she has performed that aspect successfully during training or previous competitions
- Get the gymnast to rehearse mentally the

situation as a positive performance and to repeat this until he or she can do this without self-doubt entering the thoughts.

The important thing to remember is the more exposed to the competition environment gymnasts have been the better they will be prepared to cope with the demands and situations they will encounter.

Nutritional Guidance for a Gymnast

The current climate of unhealthy eating and the increasing incidence of obesity has a high media profile and it is important to be aware that if a gymnast is overweight the possibility of injury can increase. The subject of diet is a delicate one and if you feel a gymnast may benefit from a reduction in weight then it must be handled very carefully.

It is recommended you broach the situation with tact and perhaps recommend getting the advice of a qualified dietician or nutritionist.

It is important a coach has an understanding of what constitutes a balanced diet so he or she can give advice on the basic food intake required to sustain the energy supply needed to meet the demands of training.

During the pubescent years the growing young gymnast is at his or her most vulnerable due to the many changes that are occurring in the body. The dietary intake of food and the nutrients it provides are critical to the well-being of the growing child.

The Balanced Diet for the Gymnast

Good eating habits should provide a balanced diet for gymnasts and this should contain appropriate amounts of carbohydrates, proteins, vitamins, minerals, fluid and fibre.

Sources of Energy

The energy providing nutrients are carbohydrates, fats and proteins. The typical intake of carbohydrates for a man will be around 250 to 300g per day and for a woman this will be around 150 to 300g. Typically a competitive gymnast will require between 1,500 and 2,000 calories per day but this will be more if the gymnast is training two to three times a day.

Useful facts to remember are:

- If the calorific intake exceeds the calorific expenditure the body will gain weight
- If the calorific intake matches the calorific expenditure the body weight will remain the same
- If the calorific intake is less than the calorific expenditure the body will lose weight.

Carbohydrates are the best source of energy and are best obtained from wholemeal bread, pasta, cereals, vegetables, nuts, peas and pulses such as beans. It is recommended that 50 per cent or more of the calories come from carbohydrates.

Fats are essential for the insulation of the body and are also a source of energy. However, fats contain twice as many calories as carbohydrates and it is recommended that only 35 to 35 per cent of the calorific intake should come from them.

Protein is required by the body to repair tissues and muscles but is also a source of energy. Protein is obtained from white meats (turkey and chicken), fish and low-fat dairy products.

Vitamins are essential to the bodily functions, and in particular Vitamin B as this is required in the process to release energy from the food we eat. Vitamins are obtained from foods such as vegetables, fruits, liver and dairy products.

Minerals such as iron and calcium are critical in the nutrition of the young gymnast.

Calcium is involved in the process of developing bone mass and is therefore particularly important during the periods of growth of the body. Calcium is also necessary for the repair to damaged or injured parts of the body.

Iron is a constituent of haemoglobin that is essential to the oxygen transport system of the blood.

High fibre foods such as whole grain foods, cereals and pulses assist the passage of food and waste products and are an essential part of a balanced diet.

Water is one of the most important nutrients in the diet as it is essential for maintaining the transport mechanism in the body. It controls the body's temperature, carries the nutrients to the tissues and helps remove waste products. Water absorbs the heat generated during exercise and carries it to the skin, where sweating keeps the body cool. It should be noted that just 3 per cent of body weight lost through water loss may affect performance seriously. It is recommended around 200ml of carbohydrate drink should be taken every 15 minutes to avoid dehydration and boost energy sources.

Diet and Exercise

If a gymnast is to meet the high training demands it is essential that diet and food intake are sufficient to sustain the high demands for energy. The following will provide appropriate guidelines to meet these requirements.

Pre-exercise Intake

Prior to training or competition the carbohydrate intake should be:

- 3–4 hours before training: 5g per kg of body weight should be taken
- 1 hour before the event: 2g of carbohydrate per kg of body weight and 300–500ml of carbohydrate drink
- 15–20 minutes before training: a high carbohydrate snack or carbohydrates drink.

During Exercise or Competition

To avoid dehydration and minimize fatigue 100–200ml of carbohydrate drink should be taken every 10 to 15 minutes.

Post-event Nutrition

Following intensive exercise by-products, such as lactic acid, must be removed and the energy stores in the muscles must be replenished. The process for achieving this (glycogen synthesis) is at its peak in the first 2 hours following exercise.

It is recommended that the most effective method of replenishing the energy stores is to take in 50g of carbohydrate within 2 hours following exercise i.e. 200–400 calories in the first 2 hours, and 200–300 calories in the next 2 hours.

Glycaemic Index of Carbohydrate Foods

The Glycaemic Index (GI) is a measure of how quickly carbohydrates are digested and absorbed to produce the energy source glucose in the blood. The higher the GI, the quicker will be the rise in level of glucose in the blood.

Recommended Selection of GI Foods

- Pre-training and pre-competition: eat medium GI foods
- During and immediately after training: eat high GI foods
- In the evening: eat low GI foods to avoid fat storage
- To reduce body fat: eat low GI foods.

Note: An excessive intake of carbohydrates (calories) without sufficient exercise will result in increased storage of body fat. The recommended level of daily intake of each nutrient will be provided by a balanced diet and over-consumption of mineral supplements may cause toxic accumulation that can be harmful.

Table 4 Glycaemic index of carbohydrate foods.

Low GI	GI	Medium GI	GI	High GI	GI
Fructose	23	Banana	53	Pineapple	66
Milk	30	Crisps	54	Bread	70
Yoghurt	33	Boiled potatoes	56	Watermelon	72
Apple or pear	36	Boiled rice	56	Jelly beans	80
Pasta	41	Orange juice	57	Baked potato	83
All-bran	42	Rye bread	64	Cornflakes	84
Chocolate	49	Muesli	68	Sports drinks	95

USEFUL INFORMATION

The contact details listed below may be useful to coaches within the sport of gymnastics.

British Gymnastics (the national governing body in the UK)
Address: Ford Hall, Lilleshall National Sports Centre, Newport, Shropshire, TF10 9NB.
Website: www.british-gymnastics.org
Email: information@british-gymnastics.org

Sports Coach UK (the body responsible for implementation of the National Operational Standards for coaching in the UK)
Address: 114, Cardigan Road, Headingly, Leeds, LS6 3BJ.
Website: www.sportscoachuk.org

Fédération Internationale de Gymnastique (the world governing body for gymnastics)
Website: www.fig-gymnastics.org
Email: info@fig-gymnastics.com

Simone Biles on the floor.

GLOSSARY

This is a glossary of terms and words used in this book and in gymnastics generally.

The dictionary definitions may differ from the gymnastic explanation shown below.

Acceleration   An increase in speed or velocity of a body

Accelerator   A gymnastic skill that is used to increase the speed of movement

Aerobic exercise   Exercise that requires oxygen to release the energy stored in the muscles and liver

Adenosine Tri-phosphate   The immediately usable form of energy stored in the muscles and liver

Agonist   A term used to identify the muscles that are contracting in order to move a limb

Anaerobic exercise   Exercise that does not require oxygen to release the energy stored in a muscle

Antagonist   A term used to describe the muscles that are lengthening to allow limbs to move

Arch   A body shape in which the spine is bent backward

Acrobatic elements   Gymnastic movements that include somersaults, back flips and handsprings

All around   A competition in which the gymnast competes on all the apparatus

Back flip   A backward handspring

Blind change   A half turn around one arm during a backward giant swing on uneven bars or horizontal bar

Body shape   The posture shown by the gymnast such as tuck, stretch, dish or arch

Body tension   Holding the mid-body tight to control the shape of the body

Burnout   An effect of fatigue causing underperformance

Calorific intake   The total number of calories contained in the food we eat

Carbohydrates   The main source of energy in food

Choreography   The arrangement of body movements and dance elements in a floor or beam routine

Coaching   Creating an environment that encourages and enables the gymnast to learn

Coaching process   The sequence of events that support the coaching methodology

Consistency   Being able to repeat a movement or skill accurately, over and over

Consolidation period   Time spent in training to ensure consistency in performing a skill or movement

Cool down   A series of light exercises used to commence recovery after training

Dedication   Being fully committed to something

Dietician   A person trained to advise on the content of the diet

Difficulty value   The numerical figure that is used to indicate the level of difficulty of a movement or skill

Dish   A body shape in which the body is slightly concave

Dislocation   A movement in which the gymnast swings from forward swing in hang, through the rings, into hang on the rings

Dismount   A movement used to end the routine, departing the apparatus and landing on the floor

Double leg circle   A movement on the pommel horse, where the whole body circles around the hands

Double somersault   Two complete rotations of the body around the horizontal axis

Dynamic   A powerful and fast movement or action

Element   An individual gymnastic skill or movement

Endurance   The ability to perform physical exercises repeatedly for some time before tiring

Endo circle   A forward straddle circle finishing in handstand on the asymmetric bars or horizontal bar

Extension   A movement in which the limbs of a joint are moved apart

Extrinsic motivation   The use of external rewards to motivate the gymnast

Fatigue   A point where a body or muscle runs out of energy

Feedback   Information regarding a performance communicated from the coach to the gymnast.

Flexibility   The range of movement in a joint complex

Flexion   A movement in which the limbs are brought closer together

Focus   To concentrate attention on something

Giant swing   A complete rotation around the bar with the body extended in the handstand shape

Goals   Aims, targets or ambitions

Gymnast-centred   A system or process that is focused on the gymnast's needs

Hamstrings   The powerful muscles on the rear of the upper leg

Hand guard or hand grip   A leather strap worn on the hands to provide a grip on the apparatus and to protect the hands against wear due to friction

In-location   A movement from a swing to the rear in hang, through the rings into swing in hang performed on the rings

Intrinsic motivation   Self-motivation. Motivation from within oneself

Joint   The point in the skeleton where two bones meet

Judges Officials who assess and score the gymnasts performance

Mental preparation Using training methods that allow the gymnast to visualize a movement pattern or learn how to deal with nervousness or stress

Moment of Inertia (m of i) The distribution of the mass of a body that determines the degree of resistance of the body to movement or rotation

Momentum The degree of motion gained as a result of movement. The faster a body moves the more momentum it will possess

Morale The level of confidence and spirit of a gymnast

Multiple twists More than one turn around the long axis of the body

Muscle The parts of the body that contract to cause a limb or bones to move

Nutrition The process through which the body gains benefits from the food and drink digested

Nutritionist A person who is trained to provide advice on the food we should eat

Olympic Games An international, multi-sport event that takes place every four years

Olympian A person who has participated in an Olympic Games

Optional exercises
A sequence of voluntary gymnastic skills performed by a gymnast in a routine

Overload A term used to describe a situation where the training demand is increased in order to evoke an increase in strength

Peaking Increasing the training load to a maximum at a particular point in the training programme

Physiotherapist A person who is trained to prevent injury or help you to recover from injury

Physical support Assistance to the gymnast provided by the coach

Pike A body shape in which the body is folded forward at the hips

Planche A gymnastic skill in which the body is held horizontally, supported only by the arms and hands

Positive self-talk The practice of reciting positive statements to eliminate negative thoughts

Posture The shape in which the body is held

Proprioceptive nuromuscular facilitation (PNF) A particular method used to increase the range of movement in a joint

Protein A nutrient in our food that is used to repair body tissue

Psychology The science in which the function of the mind is studied and used to train the mind

Psychologist A person who is trained to teach others how to prepare mentally or cope with stress

Pubescent growth period The period of rapid growth in young people

Ranking The order in which a gymnast or team is placed according to their scores

Rebound Movements that occur as a result of repulsion from an apparatus such as a springboard, trampette or trampoline

Rehabilitation The period of recovery following injury or illness

Release and catch A gymnastic skill in which the gymnast release the grasp on the bar, somersaults and re-catches the bar

Resistance How difficult it is to move something

Rotation A movement in which the body turns about an axis

Routine A sequence of gymnastic skills performed in a competition. Often called the 'competition exercise'

Rybalko turn A one and half turn around the long axis of the body performed from a backward giant swing on horizontal bar

Scissor or Shear A pommel horse skill in which the gymnast swings with straddled legs and under cuts one leg under the other

Self-evaluation Reflecting on and evaluating your own performance

Shadowing A method of support where the coach closely follows the movement pattern of a skill without any actual contact with the gymnast

Soft tissue Muscles, tendons and ligaments in the body

Spatial awareness The ability to orientate oneself while somersaulting or twisting

Special requirement A specified type of gymnastic movement that must be included in a routine

Spotting Physical support provided by a coach at the point of the gymnast landing

Stalder circle A straddle circle backward into handstand on the horizontal bar or uneven bars

Stamina Ability to sustain a physical activity for a long time

Start value A term used to describe the value of routine before points are deducted for technical errors

Static Something that is not moving

Straddle A position in which the legs are wide apart

Stretch reflex The response from a muscle to a rapid stretch

Stoop in A movement in which the body is folded to enable the legs to squat between the arms and under or over a bar

Tapering Gradually reducing the training load just prior to a competition

Tariff The value awarded to a vault or skill according to its level of difficulty

Thomas Flair An element on pommel horse in which the gymnast circles with his legs in splits

Torque A term used in mechanics to describe the turning moment about an axis of a body

Tuck A position in which the legs are bent and the knees are pulled into the chest

Trampette A one-metre square canvas bed, sprung take-off apparatus

Twist A turn around the long axis of the body during the performance of a somersault

Value parts Each gymnastic skills is awarded a value according to its difficulty and graded: A, B, C, D, E and F

Vitamins Nutrients in the food used to assist in the metabolism of food

Uneven bars Another term used to define the asymmetric bars

Warm-up Performing a series of light exercises to warm up the body and muscles prior to the training session.

INDEX

assymetric bars   138
 backward giant swing   143
 clear backward hip circle   139
 double forward somersault
  dismount   147
 forward giant swing   147
 Stalder straddle circle   141
 training aids   138
back flip   109
backward roll   105
backward somersault   112
 stretched backward somersault
  116
balance beam   150
 dismounting   152
 split leg backward somersault   151
benefits of gymnastics   15
Biles, Simone   189
biomechanics   77
cartwheel   99
cheating   22
child development   24
 early childhood   25
 early pubertal stage   25
 late childhood   25
 late pubertal stage   26
 post pubertal stage   26
 pre-pubertal stage   25
coach, types of   35
coaching code of conduct   19
coaching code of ethics   18
coaching philosophy   22
coaching practice   72
 allegations   72
 injury   73
 physical support   74
 safety   72
coaching process   29
coaching qualifications   7
 qualification pathway   10
 UKCC   10
coaching skills   19
coaching styles   33
 command   34
 discovery   35
 group   37
 guided discovery   34
 one on one   36
 practice (task)   34
communication   32
competitions   183
 nutrition   186
 routines   184
 rules   183
competitive gymnastics   7
confidence   40, 44
conflicts   37

endurance training   70
equality code   19
failure   22
fear   39
Fasana, Erika   13
feedback   31
forward somersault   118
 stretched forward somersault   119
foundation skills   88
 balance   93
 falling safely   88
 handstand   95
 straddled lift   96
 safe landings   89
Fragapane, Claudia   9
goal setting   45, 49, 75
gravity   79
handspring   107
horizontal bar   175
 backward giant swing with half
  turn   178
 double backward somersault
  dismount   181
 Endo circle with half turn   175
 Rybalko turn   179
 stoop in half turn to handstand   176
Keatings, Dan   29
Men's Artistic Gymnastics   7, 153
methods of learning   27
motivation   38
muscular contractions   63
 concentric contraction   63
 eccentric extension
 isometric contraction   63
Mustafina, Aliya   24
Newton's laws of motion   78
nutrition   186
parallel bars   167
 backward giant   170
 Healey turn   168
 piked double backward
  somersault   173
 swing in support   167
parents   40
Pargas, Ana   151
planning   48
plyometric training   69
pommel horse   153
 double leg circle   155
 front shear   157
poor performance   37
Purvis, Dan   155, 182
range of movement   54
responsibilities of the coach   18
rings   160
dislocation on forward swing   163
double back somersault dismount   164

in-location on backward swing   161
 strength held elements   166
swing in hang   161
role of the coach   17
 disciplinarian   18
 friend   18
 manager   18
 motivator   18
 philosopher   18
 reflector   18
 role model   17
 teacher   17
 trainer   17
 psychologist   17
rotational movement 80
round off   103
Smith, Louis   5, 8
snap up action   101
stages of learning   26
stretching   55
 active stretching   57
 ballistic stretching   56
 passive stretching   57
 PNF stretching   57
 stretch reflex   55
strength training   63
 hip flexors   66
 legs   68
 lower back   67
 mid body   65
 shoulders and arms   68
Tinkler, Amy   123
Thomas, Kristian   17, 175
training aids for tumbling   98
training programme   50
Tsurumi, Kako   183
Tulloch, Courtney   48
Tweddle, Beth   4, 8, 138
twisting, mechanics of   83
 anticlockwise with somersault
  85
 hula twist   84
 tilt twist   85
 torque twisting   84
Uchimura, Kohei   143, 160
vaulting   123
 classification of 126
 controlled landings   124
 handspring vault   127
 Kasamatsu   135
 run up and take off   123
 Tsukahara   132
 vaulting table   123
 Yurchenko   129
Whitlock, Max   6, 9
Women's Artistic Gymnastics
 (WAG)   7